First Edition copyright © 1988 by Lanny Bassham.
Second Edition copyright © 1995 by Lanny Bassham

All rights reserved.
ISBN 978-1-934324-26-4
Library of Congress 96-84757

Printed in the United States of America

Order from
Mental Management® Systems
www.mentalmanagement.com
ph. 972-899-9640

With Winning in Mind

The Mental Management® System
An Olympic Champion's Success System

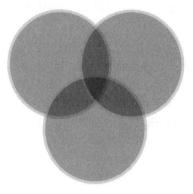

Lanny Bassham
World and Olympic Champion

Dedication

To Helen , my reason for winning.

To the Son of Man through Whom all things are possible.

To the memory of William and Natalou Bassham for the fundamental values. To my sons Brian and Troy and my daughter Heather for making me feel like a champion. To all Olympians and World Champions for their inspiration. To my students, champions all, for their passion for the mental game.

Introduction

Most people do not read introductions because they are just too darn long. So, I will make this one short. In fact, I made this entire book short, to the point, and easy to read. Are you interested in winning or helping others to win? If so, this book is written for you.

Be wary of the people no one wants on their team, the ones who are too small, too slow and not very capable. The unwanted have a built-in motivation to do whatever it takes to succeed that those who are picked first do not have. This is a story of such a person and what he did to find his place at the top of the world in his sport. I'm that person and this book is an introduction to what I've learned. I believe there is a mental system that when used will speed up the process of getting to the winner's circle.

I am well aware that there are many fine self-improvement books available. Psychologists, motivational speakers, religious leaders and business professionals write them. A competitor writes this one. The Mental Management® System is not based on psychology; instead, it is 100% based on competition. I did my apprenticeship in the arena of Olympic pressure. My credibility is not based on the courses I took in college; it's in my gold medals and the medals of my students. It's not theory; it's simply what works. My goal in this book is to share with you the mental techniques that I have discovered and used to win.

--Lanny Bassham

The Journey of a Dream

A dream is born in the mind,
a picture of what might be,
and a vision of a new and better life.
But if it stays in the mind,
it becomes a wish never to be fulfilled.

It must move on...

So the dream moves to the heart,
feelings surround it, giving it life.
But if it stays in the heart,
it becomes a "could have been,"
dying in the fire of emotion.

It must move on...

So the dream moves to the hands,
there to be put into action.
Having been given life in the heart ,
it comes to fruition through work.
But if it stays in your hands,
it becomes self-serving.

It must move on...

So place your hand in the hand of another,
and if God wills it, your dream moves on...forever.

Lanny Bassham

Contents

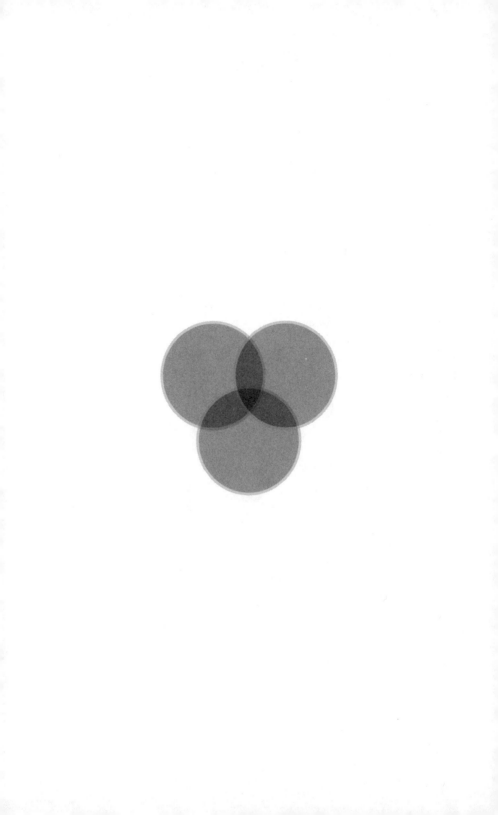

Ben Crane
PGA Tour Winner

When Fred Funk first told my wife and me about Lanny Bassham we felt like we had heard about sports psychologists before. I had read books and tried other methods of achieving mental consistency. This was different. This was someone who had gone to the Olympics and knew he was good enough to win, but didn't have the proper mental system to get the job done. So Lanny set out on a four-year journey to get back to the Olympics and shoot in a way that he would be less affected by the environment and more concerned with his personal mental program.

I have felt much of the same in big golf tournaments. I had the physical skills, but I didn't have a plan for what I was going to do when things arose in the rounds that needed mental toughness. I have been paying close attention to how I feel and react in tournaments and I have concluded like most golfers that the game is 90 percent mental. Now I want to clarify that I have put in many years of physical practice to get my skills to their current level and one of my goals is to continue to develop them much further.

But to reach my goals I knew that mental consistency had to become my goal as well. Mental Management® has shown me how to think before the shot, during the shot, and after the shot. As most everyone knows I have had issues with playing slow on the golf course. I think it's safe to say that I was a tough case when I first decided to go see Lanny and Troy Bassham at Mental Management® Systems. My mind was overactive when I was trying to hit golf shots and I would waggle over the ball until I would get so frustrated that I would just forget everything and hit the shot. Because of their help, I have come a long way in the last few years. I have started to feel the trust come up and the try go down as my mental program gained consistency.

I remember feeling this really soft, peaceful place in my mind as I was coming down the stretch trying to win my 3rd PGA Tour event. I used to try to wake myself up from that peaceful place as if to say to my Subconscious "You're not trying hard enough." Later the same year, I had a 10 foot putt to win in Malaysia, and I remember praying for peace as I walked onto the green and not feeling pull from the environment, but just a quiet very soft place. Everything just washed away, and I was just entirely focused on running a good mental program, not trying to make a result happen. The more I have committed to the process, the more I have gotten out of it. I can relate it to my faith in Jesus Christ. The more I put into knowing Him, the closer I feel to God. When I lose my dependence on Christ and start trying to do things on my time line, I begin to try; not trust. I feel my mental game is similar; when I make it primary instead of focusing on results, I have a lot more success.

With Winning in Mind is a reference book on the relationship between thinking and performing while under pressure taught by a person who has lived what he teaches.

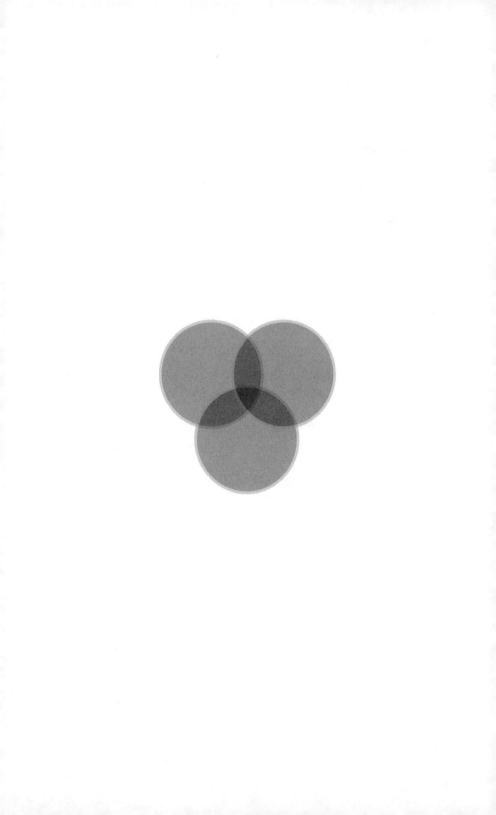

Section 1

What is Mental Management®?

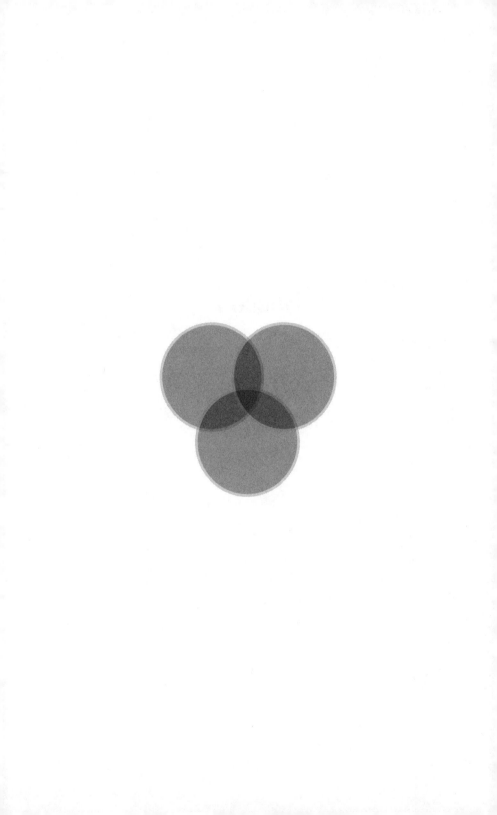

Chapter 1
It Doesn't Matter if You Win or Lose - Until You Lose.

I always wanted to be a winner. For as long as I can remember, I have loved winning. I noticed in elementary school that the kids who won the races were always the happiest. All the other kids would come up to them and say, "That was great, you're super!" But it never happened to me. I never won a race in my life. I wasn't even good enough to be average. You know what they say about average - the best of the worst or the worst of the best. Well, I was among the worst of the worst.

No one ever comes up to the loser and says, "Nice job!", unless it is a rebuke. I was always smaller, slower, and weaker than the winners. I wanted the recognition, but I was unable to earn it as an individual. So I decided to try team sports. I was the last person picked on the baseball team. I got alternate right field. If you have ever played Little League baseball, you know that they seldom hit the ball to right field. That's where you put your worst player and I was the alternate.

Memories can be painful. It's a Little League game, and I'm in right field when I hear a funny crack of the bat. A ball has been hit to me. I had never seen a ball like that before. It was smoking, heading straight for me, and I couldn't get out of the way. All I had to do was catch it and be a little bit of a hero for the first time in my life. Instead, the ball hit me right between the eyes. Two runs scored before I could throw it in. Everyone thought it was funny, but I went home in tears.

My father was a military officer and a war hero. As an only child, I wanted more than anything to make him proud of me. He was a tough guy, and I felt I had let him down. I remember telling him, "I'm sorry, Dad. I'm just no good." He said, "No, you're mistaken. There is nothing wrong with you, son. You just haven't found what you are good at yet. Keep looking. Why not try something where the balls are bigger and easier to catch?"

So the next year I tried out for basketball. The coach carefully selected the players and their positions. The guards, forwards, and center were selected. I remained on the bench. That's where I sat out the season. Again, I was the last one to play in the games, and I was beginning to develop a super-low Self-Image.

I especially remember one game. The ball got away from one of the other team's players, and it bounced toward me. This time I knew exactly what to do. I would make certain I caught the ball this time and go in for an easy lay-up. As I got to the ball, a thought crossed my mind. Is that our goal or is the other one ours? I had forgotten. In my moment of indecision, I accidentally kicked the ball out of play. I was a failure in everything I had tried, and I was ready to give up on sports.

People say that it doesn't matter if you win or lose. But when you lose, it matters, and it hurts. One day, after studying the Olympics in class, our sixth-grade teacher said, "It's possible that one of you might one day win an Olympic Gold Medal. Who do you think has the best chance of winning a medal in this class?" A boy sitting next to me stood up and said, "I don't know who has the best chance but I do know who has the WORST chance; Lanny!" That's when losing hurts, and I was losing a lot. I made up my mind that some day I would show that kid. I had to find a sport that would take a short, slow athlete to the Olympics.

One day a friend of mine invited me to a rifle club meeting.

"What do you do at a rifle club meeting?" I asked.

"We shoot rifles. It's fun, and it's an Olympic sport," he said. I was interested.

"How strong do you have to be to be a rifle shooter?"

"You don't have to be strong. The rifles aren't that heavy." He said.

"How tall do you have to be to be a rifle shooter?"

"You don't have to be tall."

"OK, how fast do you have to be to be a rifle shooter?"

"You don't understand," he replied. "You don't have to be tall or strong or fast. All you have to do to be the best rifle shooter in the world is stand still."

"Great!" I exclaimed. "There's an Olympic sport where all you have to do is be still. I can do that. I've had lots of practice in the dugout and on the bench."

That was the beginning of my shooting career. My father took me to that rifle club meeting, and they let me shoot. I wasn't good at it, but I wasn't bad at it. I was average. I had never been average at anything in my life, and I was average at this sport from the very first night. Shooting was all I talked about the next week. My dad took me to the next meeting, but when we arrived the man running the club gathered us around and explained that he had some bad news.

"I'm afraid we are not going to be able to shoot tonight. In fact, we are not going to be shooting at all. We have some trouble with using this range, and tonight is our last night." Walking out of the range with my father, I remember looking up at him.

"You know Dad. I think this is the most disappointed I have ever been in my life!"

Then my father said, "I don't want you to worry about this, son. I'll take care of it. I'm your dad. I'll pick you up from school tomorrow." The next afternoon, my father was waiting for me after school. In the back seat of our car was all the equipment needed to shoot. He'd arranged the use of an indoor shooting hall, and for the next year he taught me to shoot.

He encouraged me, became my coach, and took up the sport as well. We practiced together and became a team. You see, my father never played baseball or basketball either. He and I became best friends on that rifle range. Fifteen months after beginning shooting, I won my first national championship.

While growing up, I don't remember doing much away from the shooting range. I was too busy training. When all the other kids went to movies, I practiced. I trained an average of five hours a day, five days a week for twelve years before I made my first Olympic team. I shot on high school and college rifle teams. I would get to school early and train. Then I would train again before going home. The weekends were for matches or all-day training. This should not come as any surprise to you; all Olympians train hard. What I have learned since is that I did not need to spend that much time and effort. I did not have a Mental Management® System then. If I had, I could have done better on half of the effort and half of the time. But I am getting ahead of the story.

I vividly remember my first Olympiad in Munich, Germany. It was 1972, and my teammate, Jack Writer, was the best shooter in the world. He had won all three pre-Olympic World Cups and was the hands-down favorite to win the gold. He was National Champion, held the world record, and was the reigning World Champion. Jack had two problems. First, there is always more pressure on the favorite. I was confident that this would be problematic for him at the Olympics. He'd won the silver at the previous Olympics in the event and anything less than the gold would be disaster for him. Most people buckle under that kind of pressure. He had another problem as well: ME. I occasionally beat him in training, and it was occurring more often the closer we got to Olympic day.

I thought Jack would pressure out, and I would win the gold medal. Olympic day came. I was physically the best in the world the day of the match, but I had not planned on how the Olympic pressure would affect me. Rifle shooting is the only Olympic sport where you are trying to make the body stop. Jack and I would run three to five miles a day to force the resting heart-rate under 60 beats a minute. If you shoot when the heart beats, the movement is severe enough to cost you points. You must shoot between heartbeats. When the match started, my heart rate went ballistic, and I began to shake. I shot nine after nine. I was so scared that I lost the match in my first ten shots due to a poor mental performance. At that time, I felt like my world had ended. I'd failed my country, my family, and myself. Twelve years of training had not fully prepared me to win the gold. I lacked the mental skills. Jack Writer was the champion that day. I managed to take the silver.

Now don't get me wrong. The silver is ten times better than a bronze, and the bronze is ten times better than no medal at all. But to my way of thinking, the silver is the closest thing you can get to the gold medal and still lose. You are the world's best...loser. No one is more motivated to win the gold than the one who goes home with the silver. I set a goal to win in 1976. But I knew that to do it I needed a new mental game.

In 1972, there were no seminars in mental training like the one I teach today. In fact, the only way I knew how to learn how to cope with the mental stress of the Olympics was to question Olympic gold medalists on their mental techniques. That is exactly what I did. Over the next two years, I spent several hours daily gathering information about the mental aspect of sport. I interviewed world and Olympic champions, asking questions like: "What do you think about when you are performing?" and "What makes you able to win when others fail?"

Like the pieces of a puzzle, my mental game started to come together. I began to run the mental system I had developed. In 1974, I established the U.S. national record of 1179/1200, which stood for more than fourteen years. Also, during the 1974 World Shooting Championships in Switzerland, I won three individual world titles, eight gold medals, and with the assistance of my teammates, I set four world records.

In many ways, I was a different person. I was confident and in control. I changed mentally. I changed my Self-Image. My habits and attitudes were those of a winner. I had developed a system to control the mental aspects of my performance – The Mental

Management® System. Winning became a habit. In 1976 in Montreal, Canada, my lifelong dream came true. I won the Olympic gold medal. Then, two years later, I repeated as World Champion in Seoul Korea.

I began teaching The Mental Management® System to athletes shortly after the Olympics. I have given seminars on four continents, and the system has been translated into more than a half-dozen languages. I have had as clients the Olympic teams of Great Britain, Japan, Korea, Taiwan, India, Canada, Australia, and the United States. I have had the pleasure of presenting The Mental Management® System to Olympic athletes, PGA Tour players, doctors, attorneys, teachers, accountants, business executives, directors of sales, the Navy SEALs, Miss USA winners, Miss America finalists, the FBI, the US Marshals, and even the United States Secret Service. I've had the privilege of helping elite competitors win national, world and Olympic titles with Mental Management® and believe that this system can help you as well.

Chapter 2
Winning is a Process

In my more than twenty-five years in competition, I have been both a participant and a winner. I can tell you it is much more satisfying to win. I think everyone knows that. A fact that is not so widely known is that ninety-five percent of all winning is accomplished by only five percent of the participants.

What makes the five percent different? I've interviewed Olympic champions of every size, color, nationality, and economic status. The media would explain their success by calling it talent as if they were gifted in some special way. I know many champions that feel they are fortunate but none that admit to being gifted. Talent equals skill and it is acquired, not awarded. But skill alone will not make you a winner. Just under the top five percent are thousands of skilled participants who place high in the competition but fail to win. It's not anything you are born with – we are all born with the seeds of greatness within us. It is my observation, after competing against and teaching the world's best, the primary thing that separates the winners from the others is the way they think. Winners are convinced they will finish first. The others hope to finish first.

An example of this difference is the great Olympic shooting champion from England, Malcolm Cooper. We were in Seoul, Korea, in 1978 for the World Shooting Championships. Malcolm was favored to win the world title in the standing position, which surprised no one because he held the world record in that event. Just before the competition was to begin he said, "I'm going to win today!" It wasn't said in a bragging tone. The man was just convinced he was going to win. Then he discovered that his rifle was damaged, and he had to borrow another shooter's rifle for the match. This presented him with a huge problem. Rifles are different. The trigger pull, weight and balance differences would put Malcolm at a huge disadvantage. Then I heard him say, "Wouldn't it be something special to win this match with a borrowed rifle. That would really be something. I'm going to do it!" And that is exactly what he did, setting the world record in the process. You see the circumstances didn't matter, he expected to win anyway. That is the difference.

I am not saying that everyone who expects to win will always win. What I am saying is if it is not like you to win, you have no chance of winning at all.

When athletes have the mind-set that they expect to perform well, victory is automatically an option. For others, hope is their mind-set. Who would you pick to win that competition? I certainly wouldn't rely on hope.

Another example of a champion who expects to win is archer Darrell Pace. I first met Darrell in 1976 at the Olympics. At 5 feet 10 inches tall and only 115 pounds, Darrell didn't look like an Olympic athlete. Yet at the tender age of 19, he was already the World Champion and world record holder in archery.

I spent a lot of time with Darrell in Montreal. We met in the evenings, after our respective training sessions and talked about the upcoming event. I was fascinated by Darrell's bold attitude of confidence. He was convinced that there was absolutely no possibility that he could lose the gold medal. He referred to the gold as "my medal." He would say things like, "I wonder where they are keeping my medal," and "Everyone is after my medal, but they can't take it from me!" He had already won the gold medal in his mind.

I asked him why he was so certain he would win. Darrell's answer was, "I am more committed to mental training than any of my competitors!"

I kept thinking about Darrell as his event drew near. He had helped to reinforce many of my own attitudes on the mental game and on winning. On the day of my event, as I prepared my equipment to compete, I saw Darrell sitting next to my wife in the spectator area. "He's come to watch me win," I thought. The time for talking was over. It was time for winning. We both won gold medals that year.

The expectation of winning comes from an internal feeling the champion has concerning his performance. He is in harmony with the idea that his expectation and his performance are equal.

Over the past 30 years, I have talked to a lot of winners about winning. Some were National, World and Olympic Champions. I find it interesting that champions who were consciously trying to win while competing rarely do. You heard me right. They weren't TRYING to win the competitions.

Here is an example from the world of golf. I began working with PGA Tour player Ben Crane in 2007. Ben is a joy to work with, and we have taken on many challenges together through the years. In late 2009, Ben held a summit of his support team including his wife Heather, his agent, his trainers, his doctors, his caddie, and of course his mental coach. At this session, we evaluated Ben's strengths and the areas that needed improvement. In setting goals for the year it became evident that Ben had not won on the tour in a while. We debated the question of setting a goal to win in 2010. I noted that although I believed strongly in setting goals that wanting to win badly was one reason why Ben had not won on the PGA Tour. I suggested that instead of setting a goal to win Ben should goal set to make the process of playing well his primary focus. "Process is Primary" became a theme for the year. Ben's job while playing was to think about executing his mental and technical systems and not think about winning. Scoring is a function of great execution, and winning is the result, but thinking about winning can pull your focus off of proper execution in a competition. Thinking about process is the answer.

In the fourth tournament of the year at San Diego's Torrey Pines course Crane found himself just 30" from the cup on 18. The crowd knew Ben needed to make the putt for the win, but Crane had no idea. When the ball rolled in, his playing partner Ryuji Imada offered his hand in congratulations. Thinking this was just the customary handshake after the round, Ben did not realize he had won until Heather ran on to the green.

"Did I win?" Crane said. This was proof that a player can cause his mind to think about process instead of outcome even with the possibility of winning pulling at him. Crane's third career victory earned him $954,000 sending him on to his best year in golf to that point. Ben would win again at the inaugural Asia Pacific Classic pocketing another cool million. Ask Ben Crane if thinking about winning while playing is a good thing. I'm betting he will answer "Glorify God and Process is Primary."

I have interviewed hundreds of World and Olympic Champions and asked them what they were thinking about while performing at their best. Interestingly, most say that they were thinking about nothing or very little while winning their event. This makes sense when you consider that when the Conscious Mind is quiet the Subconscious can do its best work. We need to perform subconsciously in big competitions. When we think about winning while performing, we become outcome-oriented instead of performance-oriented and normally over-trying is the result. Over-trying has caused more good competitors to lose competitions than any other form of mental error.

It is difficult not to think about winning the competition when you are in position to win it. You cannot hide from the score if you are performing well for if you are near the lead and are "score-sensitive" someone will certainly remind you of your place. Sometimes you want to win so badly that it becomes the most important thing in your life at the moment. Ask any finalist about wanting it so badly you can taste it. But the taste is bittersweet if wanting it too much keeps you from performing well enough to attain it. Friends tell us to just go out and enjoy the competition. Yeah, right. It is easy to say but oh so hard to do. But, that is exactly what some of the people we have a difficult time beating ARE doing. They are working hard in training and working easy in the competition. This is an advantage some of our younger competitors have on us old guys. They still view this as a game. We see it as life or death and it's neither one. What winning means to each of us is a very individual thing. One thing is certain however, your worth as a person is not equal to your score this day. It is more than a game to the serious player but not worth the self-destruction that many competitors do to themselves after a poor performance.

Is there a proper time to think about winning? Well that depends on your definition of winning.

14

First, there are many winners in a big competition. There are class winners, pro and amateur winners, male-female, junior-senior-veteran winners, and team event winners. But, there is only one overall winner of the competition or should be in my opinion. This is the position that every truly competitive person wishes they held. Secondly, there are many ways to win other than finishing first on the leader board. One could argue that we win whenever we advance down the road to achievement. We win when we learn and we learn more from our struggles up the mountain than by just standing on the summit.

Winning and being a winner can be two different things as well. Did you hear about the USA Olympic shooter in Athens that shot on the wrong target on his last shot in the final and lost the Gold Medal? What was not so widely broadcast was how the shooter handled his mistake. Once he fully understood what had happened, 23 year-old Matt Emmons was the first to congratulate the winner. He took the responsibility for his error and accepted the consequences with grace and honor. You do not have to win to be a winner. One could also argue that who you become is equally important to where you finish in the long run.

So, should we be concerned at all about winning? Certainly. And the best focus, in my view, is on a winning performance, not on finishing on top. I suggest that you goal set to have a winning performance on the day of competition instead of goal setting to win the competition. What is the difference you ask?

15

If you goal set to have a winning performance you will always be process-oriented and not outcome-oriented. You will be much less likely to over-try in the competition because you are always focused on the next step and not counting your score.

I'll give you one more reason to focus on having a winning performance instead of winning the event. The player with the best performance in a tournament does not always win it. If you've been competing any time at all in events with staggered start times you have seen this happen or had it happen to you. You can draw a late start time when the weather is brutal and be beaten by someone playing in easier conditions. Who really had the better day? If you had both been out at the same time you just might have been the victor. Stay at the game long enough and what is taken away will be given as well.

Don't get me wrong. If you are first on the leader board I will be the first to say you've won the event. But, I also believe that maybe more than one person had a winning performance today and their names will not be recognized. If you are one of those competitors you can leave with your head held just a bit higher than normal and your Self-Image will grow a bit for your work this day.

There is a time to think about winning and that time is while training for the event. Your Self-Image needs to believe that it is "like you" to win. One way to enhance this attitude is to picture that you are having a winning performance every time you train. Your

Self -Image imprints that it is "like you" to win and adds to the likelihood that winning will fall within your comfort zone in the upcoming competition.

So, think about winning in training and keep your Conscious Mind on performance in the big event. By the way, thinking about losing while competing works every time.

What's your game? Golf? Sales? Shooting? Singing? Parenting? Managing? Coaching? Teaching? What percentage of what you do is mental? I have asked that question to hundreds of Olympic athletes and PGA Tour pros. They have all answered that their game is at least 90 percent mental.

The top five percent agree that elite performance is 90 percent mental. Then I ask them the second question. What percentage of your time and money do you spend on training the mental game? The answers are always similar: very little or less than ten percent. Now that just doesn't make sense. All say the mental game is 90 percent of their sport but they almost ignore training this vital area. One has to wonder why this could be so. In the past 100 years sports and businesspersons alike have become increasingly aware of the importance of the mental game. Sports psychology attempts to help athletes through applications originating from the study of psychology and research conducted by educators. Go to any bookstore, and you will find racks full of volumes designed to get you motivated, to gain influence, to have a better attitude, and to increase your sales expertise. While these books have dramatically increased the need for performers to do something about the mental game, they have only begun to tell them what to do. That's exactly what our focus will be in this book and in the information we provide through our products and personalized training. I have devoted my life to giving the mental game definition. If you can define a thing you can duplicate it. If you can duplicate it you can achieve mental consistency. If you have mental consistency you can win.

In this book we will look at defining what you need to think about to achieve mental control, how to do it, share a model of how the mind works, provide you with principles to guide you and give you tools and techniques to make your mental game work. To control performance, especially in high-level competition, you need a system to aid you in this process. The system I use and teach is called The Mental Management® System.

What is Mental Management®?

"Mental Management® is the process of improving the probability of having a consistent mental performance, under pressure, on demand."

I wanted a system that would work all the time, in competition, under pressure. This is such a system. After you read this book, you will never again have the excuse that you could not win because you were not mentally prepared. An outstanding performance is powerful. Also, an outstanding performance is easy. Only poor performance is plagued by frustration and extra effort. Think about it. When do you expend the greatest effort – when you are doing well or when you are doing poorly? When you are playing golf well, the ball goes straight down the fairway. You don't have to chase it into the rough. You do not spend time looking for the ball. When you play really well, you are balanced and in harmony with your efforts. When I won the Olympics, the actual performance seemed easy for me because I was balanced in my three mental components: the Conscious Mind, the Subconscious Mind and the Self-Image.

The Mental Management® System focuses on integrating these components, developing each to its full potential and keeping a careful balance between them. In their most basic form, these mental components are as follows:

The Conscious Mind

The Conscious Mind contains your thoughts and mental pictures. The Conscious Mind controls all of the senses: seeing, hearing, smelling, tasting and touching. It is what you picture or think about. Every time we think about something, we do it consciously. The Conscious Mind processes our environment. Its normal function is to gather information and give us options. The Conscious Mind plays a very important role in our success. Before we can expect to be successful, we first have to consider what type of success we desire. For some of us winning will have a different meaning. Some people view winning as being the best in a tournament. Others view winning in terms of reaching a personal goal or playing beyond a certain level. There are players who look at beating certain people and define that as winning. No matter how you define it, we all view winning consciously. We set goals consciously. We set priorities and establish time lines consciously. We think out our life and that is why it is so important. We tend to become what we picture. If you don't think you can be successful, you won't be. Henry Ford said it best, "If you think you can or can't, you're right."

The Subconscious Mind

The Subconscious Mind is the source of your skills and power to perform. All great performances are accomplished subconsciously, without much conscious thought. We develop skills through repetition of conscious thought until the Subconscious Mind automatically performs them. The conscious trains the subconscious. Once the skill can be performed without conscious thought it has become a subconscious skill. In most applications there are far too many parts moving at one time to consciously think about all of them. This explains why most performance applications seem difficult in the beginning. Nevertheless, with hard work and practice it is possible to master the basic skills needed to grow. Once players have developed skill and can perform these motions subconsciously it allows them to start learning advanced skills in order to take their game to the next level. In chapter 11 we will take a look at how we can build the Subconscious Mind and shorten the amount of time it takes to master skills.

The Self-Image

The Self-Image makes you "act like you." It is the total of your habits and your attitudes. Your performance and your Self-Image are always equal. This is the most important of the three, because the Self-Image and success are directly related. The Self-Image and the Conscious Mind are always in communication with one another. Every time we think about something or attempt to do something it creates an imprint that is stored in the Self-Image. The Self-Image generates a view on how you see yourself based on these imprints. I believe these imprints change the Self-Image. You may have the ability to play at a very high level but if you don't have the Self-Image that it is like you to win, you have very little chance of winning.

The Mental Management® model shows how performance is generated. The Conscious Mind examines the environment, offers solutions, sets goals and priorities, and chooses the next thought sequence. If a subconscious action is required, the Conscious Mind triggers the Subconscious Mind to perform while at the same time generating an imprint in the Self-Image. The Self-Image controls the amount of subconscious skill you will use based on what it views as being true about you. In the next chapter we will illustrate how this occurs.

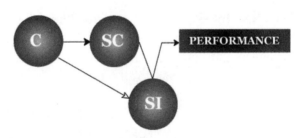

Chapter 3
The Balance of Power

Think for a minute, when you are performing your best, how much effort are you using? Great performances seem to flow. It's a wonderful feeling and has been experienced by almost everyone at one time or another. When this happens you are in what I call *The Triad State*. When the Conscious, Subconscious and Self-Image are balanced and working together, you perform smoothly, efficiently and seemingly effortlessly toward your goal. We do not always have this balance, and that is problematic.

The goal is to experience the Triad State on demand and under extreme pressure. Therein lies the challenge. Some can score well in practice, but not in competition. There is a Conscious-Subconscious connection. When we change what we picture because of the stress of competition, our body responds differently. Also, there is a Self-Image-Subconscious connection. If you think it is outside your Self-Image to do a task you may have trouble finding the skills to perform it. We desire to a consistent mental performance all the time. That is the definition of Mental Management® – the process of improving the probability of having a consistent mental performance, under pressure, on demand. Having this balance is so important that I am devoting this entire chapter to this principle.

The Principle of Balance: When the Conscious, Subconscious and Self-Image are all balanced and working together, good performance is easy.

In the Triad State, a person is balanced, confident and great performances can become a reality. It is this balance that produces power.

If a baseball player is in the Triad State, he is concentrating on the process of getting a hit, has trained so well that he is swinging subconsciously and has the mental attitude that it is "like me" to hit the ball. The result is a hit.

If a salesman is in the Triad State, he is concentrating on solving his client's problem through the sale of his product, has practiced his presentation enough so that it is subconsciously done and he has the attitude that it is "like me" to make the sale. The result is an order.

One can demonstrate the Triad State by the use of the model in Figure 4.1. In this model, all the mental processes are equal in size, and the Triad State effect occurs. Good performance seems easy. Perhaps you have experienced this feeling. It's as if nothing can go wrong. When you are balanced, you love what you are doing and have a minimum of challenges. You perform well and it seems effortless.

In fact, you cannot be beaten when you are in the Triad State, unless you face an opponent that is also in the Triad State, and who has superior ability.

However, we are often out of balance, as Figure 4.2 shows. This is a common situation when beginning any new activity. We are out of balance; we have too much Conscious process involved. Though we have good Conscious focus on the activity, we have not yet developed Subconscious skill. Also, our Self-Image tells us that we are "beginners" and cannot perform well. In this situation, the new activity seems difficult. Remember that first day in piano lessons? If we practice properly and we receive positive imprinting, our Subconscious and Self-Image circles should grow to match the Conscious circle and we will be in balance.

4.2

Frequently however, something like the situation in Figure 4.3 occurs. This is an example of a person who had trained for many years and has acquired exceptional skill, but for whatever reason, his Self-Image has not grown sufficiently. Someone who scores well in training but scores much lower in competition meets this description. This person has the skills to become a success,

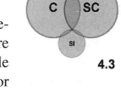

4.3

but as yet does not believe enough in himself. To perform well, this person must improve his Self-Image circle. Unfortunately, many people in this situation do not recognize that they must work on their Self-Image. They work instead on their Subconscious skill, becoming even more out of balance.

Figure 4.4 shows the balance of a person who is well trained and has a good Self-Image, but is focused on the environment around them instead of performance. The environment is a distraction. When we focus on other people, our score, or what happens if we perform poorly, we cannot focus on execution. The person in this example is like the "gunslinger" of the Old West, who had the bad habit of blowing into his barrel after each shot. Then one day while blowing he pulled the trigger. It is essential always to keep the Conscious Mind on the activity at hand or errors will result. This person must develop better concentration skills so the Conscious circle will be in balance with the others.

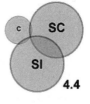

Figure 4.5 illustrates the problem of overconfidence; a trait the champion must avoid if he is to stay on top for very long. An overconfident person has an oversize Self-Image for the level of Subconscious skill he possesses. He always boasts that he will win, but he falls short

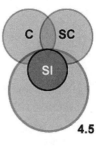

because of a lack of proper preparation. He feels that he should win because he is deserving of the title, not because he has prepared properly to win it. His imagined Self-Image is larger than his actual one. There is nothing wrong with having a big Self-Image as long as you are willing to balance it with an equally large level of Conscious and Subconscious skill.

The key point here is to learn how to make your circles larger while keeping them in balance. If you have balanced growth, you have an automatic performance increase without stress and frustration. That is everyone's aim. We all know that to become better requires effort and time. What we least want is to spend a lot of time and energy and not progress.

Every time I notice a frustrated athlete, I wonder which process is out of balance. If you just cannot seem to move ahead in your sport or business, ask yourself these questions:

Am I out of balance?

Am I concentrating on my goals?

Do I really possess the skills to do my job well?

Do I need more training?

Is it like me to do the job, or do I need to change something about me to do the work?

We are all out of balance at one time or another in our lives. To get back in the Triad State, we must grow the size of our process circles.

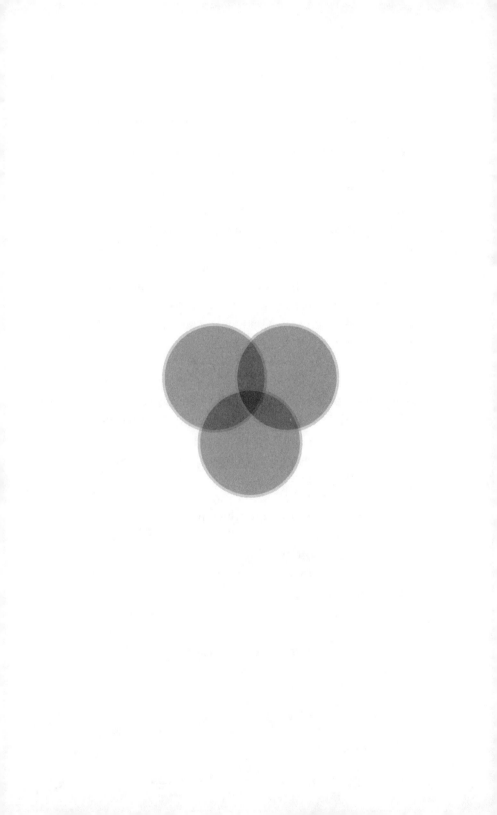

Chapter 4
Principles of Mental Management®

Gravity is an irrefutable principle of physics. We all feel the pull of the Earth on us. And just as there are proven principles of physical motion, there are also proven principles of mental success.

The Principles of Mental Management® govern how the mind works. These principles are concepts common to winners that have stood the test of time. They work for all people all the time and are applicable to sports performance, business success, and personal development. Remember, success is not an accident. Success follows a set course, and these principles are the boundaries of its path.

Principle of Mental Management® Number 1

Your Conscious Mind can only concentrate on one thing at a time.

If you are picturing something positive it is impossible, at the same time, to picture something negative. And, if you have a negative thought, you cannot, at the same time, think positively.

This is good news because it is impossible to picture playing well and playing poorly at the same time. You are either picturing something that will help you or something that will hurt you. The human mind has the capacity to control thoughts for short periods of time by personal will alone. What we picture is critical.

I remember a baseball coach telling me, "Whatever you do Bassham, don't strike out!" What do you picture when you hear, "Don't strike out?" I picture striking out. It is impossible to think about hitting the ball if you are picturing striking out. In golf for example, it is impossible for you to concentrate on the process of hitting the shot you want and thinking about outcome at the same time. If your thoughts are centered on score, or where you are on the leader board, your performance will suffer. You must keep your mental picture centered on performing well for that shot.

One way to apply a principle is to formulate and use an action statement or affirmation. This statement, written in the first person present tense, describes the action taken when applying the principle.

Action Statement for Principle Number 1

"I take control of what I picture, choosing to think about what I want to create in my life."

Principle of Mental Management® Number 2

What you say is not important. What you cause yourself or others to picture is crucial.

This is the fundamental principle of successful communication. What you actually say is not as important as the image your words convey. When the coach said, "Whatever you do Bassham, DON'T STRIKE OUT!" I pictured striking out. He set me up for failure by the way he talked to me. If he had said, "GO STRIKE OUT!" It would have had the same effect on me. Instead, he should have said, "Bassham, JUST HIT THE BALL!"

Action Statement for Principle Number 2

"I always give myself commands in a positive way. I remind myself that what others are picturing, as a result of hearing me speak, is crucial to proper understanding."

Principle of Mental Management® Number 3

The Subconscious Mind is the source of all mental power.

When you begin anything – piano lessons or your first day on the golf course – you have a lot of things to think about because nothing is automated in the beginning and good performance seems difficult. Most things, such as playing music or sports, require you to do many things at the same time. Because the Conscious Mind can only do one thing at a time, first experiences are very frustrating. The Conscious Mind needs assistance, which it gets from a second mental process called the Subconscious Mind.

After that first day of piano lessons, things begin to get easier as you develop skill through practice. Skill is defined as doing something consciously long enough for the process to become automated by the Subconscious Mind. Unlike the Conscious Mind, the Subconscious can do many things at once. In fact, your brain is like a huge computer. Just how many separate functions can be handled by the Subconscious simultaneously is hard to measure, but it may be in the billions. Your Subconscious Mind can perform a great number of activities simultaneously. That is why we need to perform in the subconscious mode rather than the conscious. It is vastly more powerful. A rifle shooter who has subconscious trigger control activates the trigger when the sights are aligned without moving the rifle. When a shooter consciously activates the trigger it is probable that the rifle will move thereby throwing off the shot.

Elite gymnasts make their very difficult sport "look" easy. If you have ever tried to pull yourself up on the rings, you immediately gain a great deal of respect for the strength needed to be a gymnast.

Their skill comes from years of training. The routines are so well learned that they are subconsciously automated. I once asked a gymnast on the U.S. team what he thought about when he performed. He answered, "I try to feel the flow of the routine. I do not want to think that any element is especially difficult or dangerous while performing." You perform best when you allow your well-trained Subconscious to do the work. However, the Conscious Mind can override the Subconscious. When this happens, performance almost always deteriorates. Sleep is a Subconscious action. If you attempt to override the Subconscious by consciously attempting to make yourself GO TO SLEEP NOW, you will probably be up most of the night.

Conscious override is a major problem for athletes on Olympic day. Instead of trusting the Subconscious Mind to perform, athletes try extra hard to do well. Conscious override is the result. You tighten up. You slow down. Off your rhythm, your performance drops. You must allow the Subconscious to do the work. Trust in your ability. Let it flow.

Action Statement for Principle Number 3

"I am so well-trained that all of my performance is subconsciously done. I trust my Subconscious to guide my performance in competition."

Principle of Mental Management® Number 4

The Self-Image moves you to do what ever the Conscious Mind is picturing.

When my daughter was nine years old, I asked her to carry a cup of coffee to a guest in our house. Then I said, "Don't spill it!" That was a bad thing to tell her. When she spilled the coffee, I should not have been surprised. After all, I put the idea in her mind. It was my error, not hers. When you say, "Don't spill the coffee." what picture is created in the Conscious Mind? I picture spilling the coffee. The Self-Image moves you to do whatever the Conscious Mind is picturing and it is picturing spilling the coffee.

It is the same in sports. There are only four seconds left in the game, time for only one more play. A touchdown is needed to win. The coach calls for his best fullback to carry the ball. He explains the play. "Now young man, you are our only hope to win this game. I want you to go out there and take the hand-off from the quarterback and run in for the touchdown. You can do it."

In goes the fullback, who explains the play to the quarterback. The quarterback says, "That's great. We are going to win as long as you don't fumble!"

Being positive is our only hope. Positive pictures demand positive results from the Subconscious. If we think negatively, we have to expect negative results.

Action Statement for Principle Number 4

"I realize that my Self-Image is moving me to perform what I am consciously picturing. I control what I picture and picture only what I want to see happen."

Principle of Mental Management® Number 5

Self-Image and performance are always equal. To change your performance, you must first change your Self-Image.

The mind is like a submarine. The Conscious Mind is the periscope. The Subconscious is the engine, and the Self-Image is the throttle of that engine. The Subconscious is always asking the Conscious Mind what it sees. Then it launches the boat in that direction. The speed is determined by the Self-Image. The Self-Image, made up of your habits and attitudes, makes you "act like you". Your Self-Image directs your behavior. This means every person has a special way of behaving. Some people like to get up early in the morning. Some people like to get up late. Some think they are good in math while science ranks high with others. Speaking before a group terrifies some people. Some people hope they can win. Some people expect to win.

We have a Self-Image about everything. It makes us who we are. The sad thing is that most people believe there is nothing they can do about their Self-Image. They believe that they are the way they are and cannot change. In fact, we are changing all the time. We experience change as we age. The direction of that change can either be determined by you or for you. If you do not take control of your life, other most surely will. I believe that one of the most important factors in success at the Olympic level is that Olympians tend to control their Self-Image growth.

Your Self-Image is like the throttle of the submarine. It controls the speed and the distance you travel. We all limit ourselves by our Self-Image. For example, it is not like me to drive my car 100 miles an hour. In fact, if I get just a few miles over the speed limit, my Self-Image makes me feel uncomfortable until I slow down. It's not like me to drive fast, so I don't.

A car salesman averages selling four to six cars a month. If after the first three weeks this month he has not sold a car, his Self-Image makes him work harder to sell four to six the last week of the month. Also, if he sells four the first week his Self-Image will slow him down to only sell two the rest of the month. It is just not like him to vary much in his performance.

We all have a comfort zone, the upper and lower limits being defined by our Self-Image. It is "like us" to operate within this zone. As long as we are in the zone, our Self-Image will provide us with extra power to improve until we are back within the zone. Likewise, if we start scoring better than our comfort zone, the Self-Image tends to slow us down until we are, once again, back in the zone. Change the zone, and we will change the performance.

Action Statement for Principle Number 5

"I am aware that my performance and Self-Image are equal. I am eager to change my habits and attitudes to increase my performance."

To change the comfort zone, we must change the Self-Image. This relates directly to the sixth Principle of Mental Management®.

Principle of Mental Management® Number 6

You can replace the Self-Image you have with the Self-Image you want, thereby permanently changing performance.

You can replace the income you have with the income you want.

You can replace the score you have with the score you want.

You can replace the *you* you have with the *you* you want.

The problem for most of us is that we know something has to change for our lives to improve but we want the change to be in other people or other things, and not in ourselves.

NOTHING IS GOING TO CHANGE UNLESS YOU CHANGE YOURSELF FIRST.

Change is a difficult challenge to face. Most of us think we are pretty good the way we are, and we resist change. Besides, it is easier for us to place the burden to change on someone else, and then it's no longer our problem. It takes commitment and effort to change. The Self-Image resists changing. Sometimes you can actually hear the Self-Image talking to you. When your alarm clock sounds early in the morning, you hear, "You're tired. Don't get up. Let's stay in bed a little longer." Your Self-Image is the part of your inner self that lets you know who you really are. It tells you things like, "What makes you think you are going to win? You've never won before. We are going to do whatever it takes to win this time."

The Self-Image is always changing, and you can direct the change or simply let your environment make the change for you. If you are proactive about controlling the direction of your life, then you must control the way you think. Every time you think about an error, you move to make it like you to create it. Every time you think about a solution to a problem it becomes more like you to solve it.

Action Statement for Principle Number 6

"I am responsible for changing my Self-Image. I choose the habits and attitudes I want and cause my Self-Image to change accordingly."

Concentration is nothing more than the control of one's mental picture. Remember, the Subconscious, with all its power, moves you to do whatever the Conscious Mind programs. If you can control the picture, you can control the performance. Our conscious picture is formed from what you think about, talk about and write about.

Principle of Mental Management® Number 7

The Principle of Reinforcement: The more we think about, talk about and write about something happening, we improve the probability of that thing happening.

This is my favorite principle of Mental Management®. Every time we think about something happening, we improve the probability that it will happen. Be careful what you think about. What do you picture? Every time you worry, you improve the probability that what you are worrying about will happen. If you are worrying about failing an exam, you are imprinting that it is like you to fail, and the

Self-Image, with all its power, will move you to make the imprint true. It is not what you want, but it is what you will get if you continue to think this way. What you must do is picture scoring well.

Also, be careful what you talk about. I've seen the following situation hundreds of times. Two shooters meet after a match. Shooter A asks, "How did you shoot?" B says, "I did terrible. I shot three nines in a row. Two were out the left for wind and the other one came because I held too long." Shooter B has just improved the probability of having nines the same way in the future because he is thinking and talking about his mistakes.

The really sad thing is that because Shooter A is listening, he is also improving the chance that he will have B's problems in the future. Be careful who you listen to. Do not spend time listening to the problems of others, or you will soon inherit their problems.

In presenting a seminar to Olympic shooters I was asked, "Mr. Bassham, in the 1978 World Championships, you shot a 598/600 to win a medal. What happened on those two nines?"

I answered, "Do you really want to know? Do you want to know how I got nines? That will not help you. You don't want to know how I got two nines. What you should be asking is how I got fifty-eight tens. Besides, I can't remember how I got the nines. I do not reinforce bad shots by remembering them."

You should talk about your good shots. By doing that you improve the probability that you will have more good shots in the future.

Be sure to write down what you want. Writing down your goal will not guarantee your outcome but it will aid the building of the Self-Image you need to be able to attain it.

Be careful not to complain. I often hear people in both business and sport, complain about their circumstances. Complaining is negative reinforcement. I teach my students not to reinforce a bad shot by getting angry. Do not reinforce a bad day at the office by complaining to your spouse. Remember something that you did well each day instead. Fill your thoughts only with your best performances, and you cannot help but be successful.

Positive Prediction: Reinforcement in Advance

People perform as we expect them to perform. There is a technique that I call Positive Prediction that is useful in increasing performance. It is a compliment given in advance of a future action. My father once told me that to obtain what you want, you must first provide someone else what they want.

I receive exceptional service at my local bank. Although I am certain the employees at my bank attempt to provide fine service to everyone, I am positive that I receive special treatment. Why? I use the Positive Prediction technique. From the very first day I opened my account, I have consistently complimented everyone in the bank, in advance, for their excellent treatment of my business. I said to the teller, "I appreciate you. You always have a smile for me when I come in the bank, and you're really good at your job." The tellers have told me they rarely receive this kind of treatment from bank customers, and they look forward to my coming to the bank. I seldom have to stand in a long line. When I come into the bank someone usually says, "Mr. Bassham, I'll open this station for you." Prediction is an attitude that says, "I expect exceptional service because you are an exceptional person."

Prediction can be harmful if used incorrectly. Eunchul Lee, the World and Olympic Shooting Champion from Korea, was a student at my International Shooting School. Several years ago, after training at my school, Eunchul was shooting with the Korean team in a competition in Mexico City. The Korean coach told me that he did not like Eunchul's prone position. He also informed me that Eunchul's attitude was poor.

I had worked with Eunchul for over a year. This coach had only met him the week before. This coach wanted to win so badly that he had the Korean shooters wound tight as a drum. Eunchul is, by nature, a very friendly and outgoing young man. His coach took this to indicate that he was not serious about his shooting. I told the Korean coach that I respected his ability and that I would look into his criticisms of my shooter as soon as we returned to the USA.

It was fortunate that Eunchul had finished his

match before the coach's prediction about his poor attitude and incorrect prone position could influence the match. Eunchul Lee won most of the medals for Korea, including a gold in prone. Later, the Korean coach came to me, apologized, and asked me to look at the prone positions of his other shooters.

When Positive Prediction is implemented correctly everyone wins. You feel great using the technique. The person you are talking to gets a lift and the results make everyone feel wonderful.

Praise: Reinforcement After the Fact

Praise good performances, and the good performances will repeat. If praising others becomes your habit, you will soon become surrounded by competent people who love to work with you.

The teachers in our local school were exceptionally considerate of my children. I called the school office to set an appointment with each of my child's teachers. When I met them they asked, "Mr. Bassham, why did you wish to see me? Is there a problem?"

"No," I replied, "I just wanted to meet you and say that you are one of the most considerate teachers in the school. I am delighted that my child has the opportunity to be in your class. I expect, now that we have met, you will not hesitate to give me a call if there is anything that we can do to aid our child in school."

Teachers are not used to hearing good news from parent conferences. It really makes their day when a parent calls in to compliment rather than complain. How much better would you do your job if you were praised more often?

Praise is an attitude that says, "I recognize exceptional service because you are an exceptional person."

Action Statement for Principle Number 7

"I choose to think about, talk about, and write about what I wish to have happen in my life."

Section 2

Building the
Conscious Circle

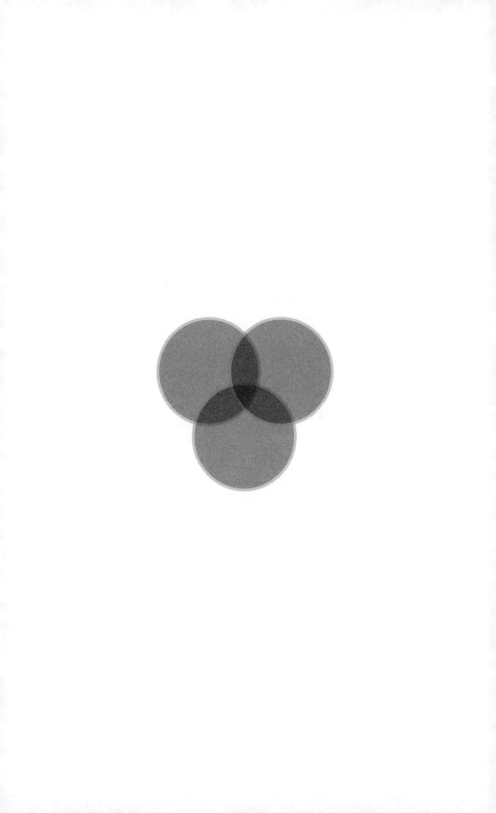

Chapter 5
The Mental Management® Goal Setting System

So, what are your goals for this season? If you haven't set them there is a good chance that you will be beaten by someone who has. Goal setting is a common practice among the winners. We are going to look at goal setting in this chapter, why it works for some and is ineffective for others. Then, I will give you a goal setting system that works.

Goal setting is not easy to do and here is why. First, there are two common methods of setting goals that most people try and neither of them work; realistic goal setting and big-sky.

Some people believe that you should always attain your goals so they try to set realistic goals. This means they will look at what they did last year and move up the scoring a bit and that will be their expectation for this year. Sound good? I don't know a single Olympic Gold Medalist that used this method successfully. Why? Because there is nothing realistic about winning a Gold Medal in the Olympics or setting a world record or reaching a dominant status in your sport. Big goals are more irrational than realistic. If you want to be realistic you had better keep your goals low. Do that and you will be beaten so often that you will soon begin to doubt the system and abandon it. I see this happen all too often. Another variant of this system is to be vague in defining your goal. "I want to shoot better this year!" Really? What does BETTER mean?

OK, so let's just do the other system. I call it big-sky. The advantage of this system is that there are no upper limits to the goals. "My goal is to win every competition this year, breaking all of the records and beating everyone." You've got to admit this sounds appealing. Who wouldn't want to have a year like that. If you try this system you are almost guaranteed to miss your goal. Most people who have banner years rarely, if ever, anticipate that it would happen just that way. The BEST years of the BEST players are rarely foreseen in advance. Why? I believe it is because the elite are not thinking about outcome. They are thinking about process.

Both of these flawed goal setting systems are outcome oriented and that is the big problem. The focus is on score or winning the competition. It should be on the process of getting a score that can win the competition. Once you take your mind off of your score and focus on the process of performing well, you are dealing with something you alone can control. You cannot control what it will take to win a competition. You cannot control what other competitors do and often you cannot even predict with accuracy what score will win a competition. But you can predict process. Process is what you can control and only what you can control. Process can be defined and anything that can be defined can be duplicated.

You can predict and control how many days a week you train. You can control the discipline of your efforts. You can control what you choose to think about and do. You can control the competitions you enter and how you choose to train for them. You can control who your teachers are and the training systems you use. My advice is to only set goals on things that YOU can control. Keep your focus on you, not your competitors. Rehearse in your mind the process of executing a combination of mental feelings and technical moves that get results. Your success is determined by how well you can control what is in front of you not by worrying about outcome.

Most books on goal setting are outcome oriented and I have a problem with that. I have no problem with setting a goal to have a winning performance, move up in a class or to make a team if you are setting the goal to identify the process of attaining the goal. Perhaps we should define attainment because attainment and accomplishment are not the same thing. Accomplishment is all about outcome and it is important. We determine who wins by accomplishment. It is the score, the color of medal and your place on the list of competitors at the scoreboard. What it does not measure is what you've learned or your growth as a competitor. It does not measure who you have BECOME.

Attainment is the total of accomplishment and

becoming. Accomplishment is how you measure the EXTERNAL and becoming is how you measure the INTERNAL. Winning is more than just a way to measure the outcome. It also reflects who the person has become. It is a mirror to life; a snapshot of who this player is as well as how high he can score. We compete on the field as we compete in life. We become competitors. We become A-class or Master-class. We don't just shoot Master-class scores. Attainment, consisting of becoming something, should be our goal not simply accomplishment.

You do this by goal setting for both what you want to accomplish AND who you wish to become in the process. There's that word again; PROCESS. If you goal set to move up to elite levels this year also ask yourself "Who do I need to become along with what I need to accomplish for this to happen?" This will help you to look at more than score and to determine the things you need to change about you to reach your goals. Perhaps you need to develop the attitudes that you need to succeed and not just the skills. Do you need greater control over your attitude in adversity? Winning is the total package. It is control over both the mental and physical processes. We become skilled. We become confident. We become champions.

Setting goals help you plan and that's beneficial but there are dangers to avoid as well. One mistake that many people make is to equate their worth as a person with whether they reach their goals or not. If the goal is reached then I am a successful person but if I miss the goal then I'm no good. If I make an A I am an outstanding person. If I get a C I'm average and a failure if I get an F. Your value as a person is more a function of your character, your beliefs and your actions towards others than your results on the playing field.

It is best to set goals for more than one year. For example, you want to win the US Open. Goal set to win the US Open within the next two years. This takes just a bit of pressure off of having to do it ONLY this year. Think about it. Who cares what year you did it. What is important is that you did it. By giving yourself two years you just might avoid trying too hard this year at the Open and that might be just enough of an advantage to give you the title.

Goal Setting System

A habit that separates the top five percent of competitors who win from the other 95 percent who just play is the practice of carefully setting goals. Most people never set them. No surprise there. However, every major corporation sets goals. Every government set goals. Every builder who builds has a blueprint. Every banker has a written contract on how the borrower is going to pay back each loan. But among individuals, normally only the super successful ever bother to set personal goals and plan their work.

Many years ago, one of my sons asked me if I would buy him a Ferrari for his high school graduation present. He knew my answer as he asked the question. I took the opportunity to show him how to set goals by asking him some important questions.

"Son, exactly what is your goal?"

"I want you to buy me a new red Ferrari sports car with brown leather seats."

"When do you want it?"

"Graduation Day."

"Why should I do that?"

"It would make your son very happy."

"What do you suppose would be the obstacles to my getting you that car?"

"$125,000 more than you had planned to spend on me."

"So, the only way I have of obtaining that amount of cash is to sell our home or something that valuable. Can you think of any other way?"

"No, Sir."

"Son, do you think the joy I would receive in getting you that car is worth my doing it?"

"No, Dad."

"You are a smart young man."

"Thanks, could I have a drum set instead?"

Are your goals just pipe dreams? Are your goals set too high or not high enough? There is a process I have learned from my Olympic training experience that you can use to set your goals just right. I call it the Mental Management® Goal Setting System.

Step Number 1

Determine a goal worth trading your life for.

My grandfather was a mail carrier in the central Texas town of Comanche. As a young teen I loved to help him deliver the mail out in the country because he would let me drive. Grandad taught all his grandkids to drive a car. He did not seem to mind if we ran over things and his old Ford sedan had the dings to prove it. He made us feel grown up and there was always a Dr. Pepper and a bag of peanuts as a treat at the end of the route. When I was in my first year of college he had a heart attack while visiting us. It was something he was not able to overcome. At the hospital we were all allowed some private time with him and I knew it was probably the last time I would be with him. As I sat down next to his bed he gave me some sound advice that has been with me all my life.

"Lanny, as I face the end I regret that I've never done anything in my life that a typical person couldn't have done. I always made the safe choice, never taking a risk. I've never been out of the state of Texas. I've never competed in anything, joined anything or built anything. I've done a good job of dodging the perils of life but in the process I missed a part of living. Don't let caution keep you from experiencing life. Go out and find a dream worth trading your life for because in the end, that is what you are doing. Set big goals. You do not want to end up regretting your life."

That was the last thing my grandfather said to me.

This goal setting system is designed for the big goals of your life. Find goals that excite you. You must be specific. The more you can identify exactly what you want, the better your chances of obtaining it.

Step Number 2

Decide when you want it.

Putting a time limit on your goals helps you to formulate a plan to achieve them. If your goal was to save $1,000 in 1,000 days, you could do that by putting a dollar a day in the bank. If you change the time limit to $1,000 in one month, the plan would have to change.

Step Number 3

List the pay-value.

Why do you want the goal? List all the reasons that are important to you for achieving the goal. Make certain the goal you set is big enough to be life-changing for you. People are motivated by three things: promise of gain, fear of loss and recognition. Set a goal big enough to move you to change your habits or attitudes. If it is too small it will just not be worth it for you to make changes in your life.

Also, the goal must be your goal, not the goal of another. Is the pay-value personally rewarding to you? I had a friend in college, a pre-dentistry major, who did not want to be a dentist. His grandfather and father were dentists, and the family expected him to join the profession. He hated school as a result.

If the pay-value is not personal, you will not act on your plan.

A few years ago, my wife told me she needed new bedroom furniture. She knew exactly what she wanted. Helen provided me with the specific brand, style and number of pieces she desired.

"Helen, this is expensive stuff," I said, "Where am I supposed to get the money to pay for it?"

She replied, "You're the big goal setter. You'll think of something." Several weeks passed, and I had completely forgotten about the furniture. I didn't want new bedroom furniture. Helen did. It didn't bother me that the drawers stuck, the finish was scratched and the mirror had a small crack in it. I just kept the light out in the bedroom. When Helen asked how the project was coming along, I said, "I'm working on it." The next weekend I returned from doing a seminar out of town and Helen picked me up from the airport. She presented me with several bright new $20 bills.

"Helen, what's this for?" I asked.

"Remember what you tell your students: To get

what you want, you have to get rid of what you don't want!"

"Sure," I said.

"Well, I sold our bedroom furniture. Here's your half."

When we arrived home I discovered I had new pay-value. Our mattress was on the floor and my underwear was in cardboard boxes up against the wall. Now every time I went into the bedroom I was reminded that I needed to act on the goal. Helen increased the pay value to me. Helen's goal became my goal. I had to get the new furniture. But I didn't have the money.

That weekend I attended a shotgun tournament. I overheard a conversation concerning furniture and guns. I met Dave Funes, the furniture king of Seattle who sometimes traded new furniture for used guns. I was shooting my Krieghoff Model 32 that I'd bought and dearly loved to shoot. Dave kept eyeing my Krieghoff as we talked. In fifteen minutes, a deal was negotiated. I would receive new bedroom furniture in exchange for a Mental Management® seminar and my shotgun. This true story illustrates another important point; there are always solutions if the pay-value is great enough. You might have to look beyond the obvious to find them. By the way, later I replaced that Krieghoff.

Step Number 4

Honestly evaluate the obstacles in your way.

Again, you must be specific. What must you do to overcome each obstacle? What habits and attitudes must you change to reach your goal? Remember, nothing is going to get better until you get better. You must change. What new skills do you need? How much additional time must you invest? What are you willing to give up?

Step Number 5

What is your plan to get your goal?

The difference between a wish and a goal is that a goal has a written plan to get it. Wishes usually do not come true. Goals with written plans have a much better chance of being reached. In Step Number 4, you identified several reasons why you were unable to meet your goal. Prepare a written plan to overcome each obstacle. Now the price you must pay for the goal becomes clearer. Planning saves time and provides direction. Do not be surprised if you cannot always see the obstacles in your way. Life has a way of adding challenges once you are on your way. Remember also that you cannot always see all of the opportunities at the start. Doors have a way of opening for you if you look for them.

Step Number 6

Evaluate your plan before you proceed.

Ask some questions.

How will going for this goal affect my priorities in life?

How will the people I care about be affected by this plan?

Is the plan consistent with my fundamental values?

Do I really believe my plan will work?

Do I really believe I can work the plan?

Is the prize worth the price?

This is the most important step in the goal-setting process. Ask yourself, "Is the pay-value worth the price I have to pay for it?" If the answer is positive, chances are your goal and plan are correct. If the plan and pay-value do not match, you must change something. Maybe you need to change the goal, the time limit or the plan.

Step Number 7

Schedule your plan.

We often fail to remember that scheduling is a vital art of the planning process. Put your plans on a calendar. I use both a large monthly calendar on my office wall and technology provides me with a calendar on my computer and phone. If the goal is not scheduled, it will not get done. Goals written down in your handwriting makes you more accountable to the goal.

When my daughter was young, she overheard me saying, "If it is on the calendar it will get done." The next day I saw marked on my calendar in crayon words, "Buy Heather a stuffed animal." What do you think I did?

Step Number 8

Start Now.

You are now ready to go. Begin right away. Do not hesitate. Do you really believe things will get better if you wait to get started? Clear the deck of time wasters and execute the first step of your plan right now. Put out high-quality effort, consistently over time, and you can do anything you consistently dream of doing.

Step Number 9

Prior to reaching your goal always set a new one to take it's place.

The day I received my Olympic gold medal was both wonderful and traumatic for me. The award ceremony was great. Hearing my country's national anthem being played while the flag was raised high in front of me was the best of feelings. However, later that day, I had an unexpected experience. I suffered severe depression, and I didn't know why. Helen recognized the problem and helped me understand that I had lost my goal. I had not goal set beyond the Olympic Games, and I was momentarily without direction. Once I set a new goal, I was again at peace.

Step Number 10

Hold on to the end or trade up.

Early in my career, I set a goal to win the national title in the air rifle event. I thought that it would take a 380 out of 400 to win. In the match I was down nineteen points with three shots left to go. I shot a nine. Now I figured, I had to shoot two tens, to win. I shot another nine. I was down below 380. I rationalized that I could not win, so I mentally gave up. I quickly put up the rifle and shot an eight. I finished with a 377. That year the national championship went for a 378. Had I been persistent, I would have won the title. Stay with your plan until it is finished. By the way, counting my score while shooting was the mental error that got me into trouble in this example.

There is one acceptable reason to let your goal go; you trade up. Do not be surprised if on your way to one goal you discover another that means more to you than the one you are working toward. If you trade up to the new goal you should view the first goal as having completed its purpose. Finding a new goal that means more to you than the first one is very rewarding but be cautious not to trade your current one for one that is easier to reach. If you do, you may regret the choice.

Case Study

Linda Thom is a pistol shooter from Hamilton, Ontario Canada. At age 8, she was taught to shoot by her father. In 1970, she competed at the World Shooting Championships in Phoenix, Arizona and finished in the Top 10. This, by the way was my first world championships. Despite Linda's achievements, she decided to focus her attentions elsewhere, taking a 7 year break from shooting. In 1982, it was announced that the Ladies Pistol Match would be an Olympic event at the 1984 Los Angeles Olympics. I met Linda at a clinic I presented for the Canadian National Team in February of 1983 in Toronto. One thing I said to her was that you must write your goals down to reinforce them.

One of the most important things I've found useful is to write out the goal in the first person, present tense. I told her to write, "I am the 1984 Olympic gold medalist in Ladies Match Pistol. Write it out in your journal every night, be disciplined to stay with it, and one of two things will happen, either you won't believe it and you'll stop writing it, or you'll keep on writing it and you'll succeed." It really works. Although Linda had a journalism degree, she didn't particularly like sitting down and writing out her goals but she did make the effort. For 18 months she wrote that she was the Olympic Champion every single night in her journal, and it came true. She told me it helped her build her Self-Image as a champion.

Linda came back to the sport with a single goal in mind; win the Olympic Gold medal. She did just that and became the first woman to win the Ladies 25m Pistol Gold Medal. What makes this even more special is that Linda's win also marked the first gold medal by a Canadian since 1968 and the first female individual gold medalist since 1928.

Chapter 6
Rehearsal: The Most Versatile Mental Tool

English is a versatile language because we have so many ways to say the same thing. According to Stanford University "mental imagery, also called visualization and mental rehearsal, is defined as experience that resembles perceptual experience, but which occurs in the absence of the appropriate stimuli for the relevant perception." I hope you got all that. Now, let me translate it into simple language. Imagery, visualization and mental rehearsal are common ways to refer to the process of thinking about an action without physically doing it. In this chapter we will look at this mental tool, why it works and why it is the most versatile and often used mental tool.

I like the term rehearsal over visualization or imagery just because it is a simple term. Many good things lose their meaning if the terms used to describe them seem complex. Rehearsal is not complex in the way I am using it. All of us have used rehearsal. Remember rehearsing your lines in the school play, that Bible verse you had to memorize or the first lines of a speech that you had to make in school. Children are experts at rehearsal and without ever being taught they can visualize winning races, slaying dragons and becoming champions. Thinking about doing a task is much easier to do than actually doing it. I won the Olympics thousands of times in my mind before entering the competition in Montreal in 1976.

There is no perfect way to do it. Some clients have told me that they see vivid colors and hear sounds that the world slows down and becomes clearer. Well, I cannot relate to that. My rehearsal is a little blurry and I do not hear sounds at all but it took me to the Olympic Gold anyway. I am open to the idea that the more vivid your rehearsal the greater the effect. I also believe that the more often you rehearse the more effective it becomes but I do not think that you have to see colors or sounds to be able to have effective rehearsal. It can be done in a few seconds or take minutes or even hours to complete. You can do it on or off of the field, while you are exercising, sitting up or lying down, while you are waiting for someone or for something to occur. It is not only easy to do but it is FREE.

Rehearsal aids the performer in executing a desired action or move with precision. Dog Agility handlers and Practical Pistol shooters use rehearsal when they are walking the course to not only improve their ability to remember the course but also to maximize their mastery of movement during the run. In addition, we teach our clients to rehearse the run several times just prior to entering the course and again after the run. I was interested in knowing why this works and after a bit of research I discovered that when you vividly rehearse an action neural pathways in the brain are created. These pathways are similar to small tracks engraved in the brain cells that can ultimately enable an athlete to perform the actual task. Therefore, one of the benefits of rehearsal is that it actually paves the roadways that we must travel to perform a desired task. (Porter, K., Foster, J. Visual Athletics. Dubuque, Iowa: Wm. C. Publishers, 1990)

Shane Murphy, one of the sports psychologists at the Olympic Training Center while I lived in Colorado Springs along with Robert L. Woolfolk and Mark W. Parrish conducted an interesting study related to performance and rehearsal. Here is the abstract of the study.

An investigation was carried out to evaluate the effect of imagery instructions on a simple motor skill accuracy task (putting a golf ball). Thirty college students were blocked on their putting ability and randomly assigned within blocks to one of three experimental conditions: (a) positive imagery, (b) negative imagery, and (c) control. Subjects in the two imagery conditions were given the identical instructions for imagining the backswing and putting stroke. In the positive imagery group, subjects imagined the ball going into the cup, while subjects using negative imagery visualized the ball narrowly missing the cup. Subjects in the control group putted without instructions. On each of 6 consecutive days, a 10-putt trial was conducted for each subject. There was a significant effect on performance improvement. Analyses showed significant differences among all groups, with positive imagery producing the most improvement, the control condition producing less, and negative imagery resulting in performance deterioration.

Is this proof that rehearsal (positive imagery) works? Sure looks like it. I think that it is interesting that the negative imagery group's performance actually went down over the test period while the positive rehearsal group's performance increased. I have observed this occurring repeatedly with my clients over my 35 years as a performance coach. Not only does positive imagery increase performance but when we think about creating error we improve the chance of error occurring as well. When we worry that bad things might happen to us we are actually rehearsing them. We are building new neural pathways toward failure.

Rehearsal is mental practice and it has many advantages for the performer. First, you are mentally duplicating everything you do when you are in action without leaving your chair. The rifle shooter, as an example, does not have to buy bullets, targets, or wear out his equipment. He does not have to clean up the range or clean his rifle when finished. And it's cheap. It costs absolutely nothing. And you can do it any time. Also, by rehearsing only good performances there is no negative reinforcement. Mental practice is a bargain and done correctly it is powerfully effective.

You can imagine far more than you currently can achieve. If you consistently rehearse what you want to achieve, what you imagine can become reality. Let me give you an example. Back in the 1970s, I was shooting good kneeling scores and began approaching the national record of 396/400. I wanted to set the record at 400, a perfect score. But I had never actually fired a 400, even in training. Nonetheless, I vividly rehearsed shooting the first 100, then another and another. I visualized each of the last ten shots building toward the record. I rehearsed what I knew would happen at that point: I would realize that I was above the record. Next, I rehearsed hearing a voice say, "That's OK, I do this all the time," Then I imagined shooting the final ten easily and saying to myself, "Another 400, that's like me."

I rehearsed this sequence several times a day for two months. In my first competition since beginning the rehearsal, I started with a 100 kneeling. My next two targets were also 100s. I began my last series with ten, ten, ten, ten. Only five more to go. Ten. Ten. Ten. Then reality set in. I was above the record. I heard an internal voice say, "That's OK, I do this all the time." I shot two additional tens, setting the national record at a perfect 400.

Principle of Mental Management® Number 8

The Self-Image cannot tell the difference between what actually happens and what is vividly

67

imagined.

The imagination is an extremely powerful part of your mind. By rehearsing a 400 kneeling, I convinced my Self-Image that it was like me to shoot a 400 kneeling. When it is impossible to get to a range, a shooter can also use rehearsal to simulate training. While in the Army from 1976 to 1978, I was assigned to a non-shooting position at Ft. Sam Houston, Texas. It was 250 miles from my home to an international shooting range. I was able to actually shoot on a range only 6 days during those 2 years, 3 days to win the Nationals in 1977 and 3 days to win again in 1978. Though I could not actually go to the range, I did continue training. Five times a week after my family had turned in for the night I simulated shooting for 2 to 4 hours in a spare bedroom, a technique called dry firing. I made the U.S. international team in 1978 and won the World Championships that year in Seoul.

Mental practice alone cannot replace good range training, but it serves as an effective supplement when actual training is not possible because of weather, injury, money or time limitations.

When NASA trains a space shuttle crew, more than half of the training deals with what to do in case of contingencies. Once launched, the shuttle cannot return to base if problems arise. Problems must be solved in advance. An Olympic athlete must perform well on a particular day or set of days. If you have an off day you do not get another chance for 4 years. You must be prepared for every contingency.

In the 1976 Olympics, I was very calm because I had rehearsed over and over every possible thing that could happen in the match and how I should respond. I was confident that I had planned for every possible contingency, which reduced my stress level, allowing me to shoot well.

Rehearsal and Relaxation

In 1976, during my final competitions leading up to the Olympics, I had the pleasure of working with Eva Funes, one of America's finest shotgun shooters. Eva's husband, David, related to me that she was unable to sleep the night before major competitions. Poorly rested, she was unable to shoot well the next day. If she took sleeping pills, her reflexes were impaired. David asked if I knew of a Mental Management® technique that would help her.

I told Eva that as long as she was going to be awake all night anyway, she might as well do something productive with her time. I told her to relax in bed and rehearse that she was shooting well in the match. When Eva began to rehearse shooting well, her level of arousal dropped, allowing her to sleep. The next day, Eva Funes, rested from a good night's sleep, won the competition.

Using Rehearsal to Improve Test Scores

Mary is taking her final exam tomorrow in college algebra. She is frantic, knowing that a poor grade on the final will result in failure for the semester. Recalling a previous history of poor math finals in high school, Mary says, "I have no chance to pass that test." With that attitude, Mary has little chance of passing her class. Mary is not in control of what questions will be on the exam but she is in control of her attitude. Mary should rehearse that she is in the classroom, taking the exam and the answers are coming easily to her. Rehearsal will not improve your knowledge or your skill level but it may improve your chances of using what you do know in a stressful situation. Rehearsal is no ironclad guarantee, but it can improve your chances of success. You may effectively use rehearsal to help you get through a negotiation, an audition, or an important presentation.

Using Rehearsal to Improve Attitude

Rehearsal can dramatically improve your attitude about your performance and how you want to feel during the competition. Have you ever started a competition feeling nervous and uncertain? How did this affect your score? Chances exist that your scoring suffers until you get used to being in the competition. Some have called this settling down. Does it take a few mistakes for you to settle down? This is not acceptable and is 100 percent avoidable if you do the correct kind of rehearsal just prior to starting the first stage of the competition. We will call this form of rehearsal Mental Attitude Rehearsal because that is exactly what you need in the beginning and at critical times during a competition when loss of the appropriate attitude can cost you.

Let's look at how this works. This form of rehearsal differs significantly from the kinds we referred previously because it is not about how you perform or even about the outcome. This is about how you want to feel while competing. It is a three-step process.

Step one: First you must define the situations where your attitude needs to be maximized.

Step Two: Decide what attitudes you need in these situations.

Step Three: Rehearse that you are in these situations and feeling the way you desire to feel.

Let's look at an example of a situation that my clients have identified that potentially cause trouble for performers. The first stage of the day is 30 minutes away. You need to be mentally ready to execute. The attitude you need to have is that it is "like you" to have a strong start. You want to feel calm, confident and in control. You need to feel comfortable performing your assigned task. You desire a strong start without over-trying. I suggest that you take a few minutes in some private place to rehearse feeling this way when you get on the course, stage or field. Then rehearse nailing your performance and see if this doesn't make a difference in your having a good start. Most performers are not aware of this use of rehearsal. You can rehearse how you wish to feel out there and when you do, you improve the chance that it will happen. Isn't that what you want?

One last comment about rehearsal is required. Because many competitors often use video as a training tool there is a slight tendency to rehearse the execution as if you are watching it on video. This technique is called visual rehearsal. When you rehearse seeing what you would actually see during the execution the technique is called actual rehearsal. The advantage of actual rehearsal is that you can feel your performance using as many of your senses as possible to make the rehearsal more meaningful and vivid. I am not against using video as long as you are watching what you are doing well much more often than reviewing your errors.

Call it what you will, visualization, imagery or rehearsal. Just remember to use this most versatile of mental tools often.

Chapter 7
The Three Phases of a Task

To properly implement the Mental Management®
System, you need to understand that everything
we do has three parts or phases:

1. The Anticipation Phase
2. The Action Phase
3. The Reinforcement Phase

The anticipation phase is what you think about
immediately before you perform. The action phase is
what you think about as you perform. The reinforcement phase is what you think about immediately after
you perform. The difference between the champion
and the average player lies in the edge the champion
gains in the anticipation, action and reinforcement
phases of performance. Champions carefully prepare
for their tasks, concentrate properly while performing, and reinforce all good results while correcting
errors. It's important to understand what these phases mean so that you'll understand how certain techniques I mention later can work for you.

The Anticipation Phase

In 1972, as we were packing to journey to Munich, Germany for the Olympics, my teammate Jack Writer approached me with an idea. Both of us were taking two rifles to the games, a primary and a back-up. Jack suggested that I put his back-up in the gun box with my primary rifle, and he would put my back-up rifle in his gun box with his primary rifle. His idea was that if something happened to one box we could both shoot in the Olympics. When we arrived at the range in Munich, my gun box was missing. It was recovered, in the locker of the Soviet weight-lifting team, just one day before the competition began. Because of Writer's idea I was able to train at the Games with my back-up rifle and shoot my primary rifle in the competition.

The bottom line is that success is no accident. Paying proper attention during the anticipation phase can make your goals easier to accomplish.

The Action Phase

During the 1974 World Shooting Championships in Switzerland, I learned a valuable lesson concerning the action phase. I was a Texas boy, stationed in south Georgia. I had trained that year in temperatures between 50 and 100 degrees. We had the final tryout and national championships at Phoenix, Arizona in June. I won the tryout in temperatures above 100 degrees.

It was August in Thun, Switzerland, and the snow was falling when the World Shooting Championships began. The temperature was four degrees Fahrenheit, and I was bone-chilling cold. I had never shot in snow in my life. I was shooting the 300-meter event. The snow was falling so hard I could not see the target. During the preparation phase of the first stage I was certain they would postpone the match. Then I heard the range command, "Commence Firing." The match started. I still could not see the target for the snow. I was frustrated. Just then I heard the shooter next to me shoot. I couldn't believe it. What was he shooting at? As I looked downrange I saw that, for an instant, the snow parted and the targets became visible. The Swiss shooters are experienced in shooting under these conditions. I had no time to become an experienced snow shooter. If winning was possible that day I had to shoot as if I had lived in the mountains all my life. So I said to myself, "I am the best snow shooter on this range. I shoot in the snow all the time. I love shooting in the snow." I watched the Swiss shooter next to me. Every time he readied to shoot, I would follow his lead. I won the match that day by adapting instead of giving in to problems.

Sometimes when your best is not good enough, you have to do what is required to win.

Every sport has its own action phase. Some are

short. In golf, the action phase starts when the club head moves, ends when the ball is beyond the control of the player and only lasts a second or so. A player will repeat this phase on every golf shot of a round of golf. Other sports have longer action phases. A marathon runner has one action phase but it is hours long. Every sport has a primary action phase and every performer has an optimum thing or series of things to think about during his action phase.

The Reinforcement Phase

I have discovered in my many years as a mental coach that most world-class athletes do well in the anticipation and action phases. However, they often break down in the reinforcement phase. I see far too many athletes reinforcing their bad performances by thinking and talking about them. Every time you talk about a bad performance, you improve the probability of having another one just like it in the future. I was very fortunate. During the years I competed for the United States, the best shooters in the world were Americans. To win, I had to defeat my teammates. Jack Writer (World and Olympic Champion), Lones Wigger (World and Olympic Champion) and Margaret Murdock (World Champion and Olympic Silver Medalist). One thing I especially remember about training with them was that they never talked about their failures in front of me. If Wigger had a problem, he kept it to himself. I asked him about that once.

He said he didn't want to give any of us an edge. He once told me, "Bassham, you will likely beat me four out of five times that we shoot against each other, but I plan to make my one time count." He was the toughest shooter in big competitions I ever faced.

Jack Writer was a talker. It was not that Jack bragged on himself, although I can understand how those who didn't know him would think that. Jack just liked to talk. His favorite subject was shooting and he kept his comments on what he was doing well. No matter how many low scores he shot, Jack would only talk about the high ones. The important lesson here is that Writer never reinforced a bad performance by talking about it and rarely shot a low score in a big match.

Margaret Murdock rarely talked at all, at least not to me. If she did, it was to compliment other shooters on their performance. I wonder if she knew that every time she praised another shooter, she also improved her own chances of winning? All three of these champions excelled in the reinforcement phase, each in their own unique manner.

To prepare yourself for competition, you need to ask yourself, how well prepared are you for your task? Are you performing below your potential because you are not properly prepared? Truthfully answering these questions will help your anticipation phase preparation. Then, ask yourself how well do you perform when the circumstances are different from those you have anticipated? This gives you insight into your action phase preparation.

Finally, ask yourself what do you reinforce? Do you praise others when they perform well? Do you praise yourself? If you have a bad shot do you focus on correcting it instead of getting angry at yourself? If you can answer yes to these questions, pat yourself on the back and continue reinforcing your successes. If not, it's time to start.

Chapter 8
Running a Mental Program

To become the best rifle shooter in the world, you only have to do two things:

Number 1: Perform well enough mentally and technically to score a ten.
Number 2: Repeat Number 1.

The same principle applies to any repetitive sport. You must be able to perform both technically and mentally in order to be consistent. If you are not consistent in your play you will lose to players who are playing consistently well in both of these areas. Winning requires you to develop a consistent mental picture. The best way to achieve this kind of concentration is by running a mental program.

The mind is very much like a computer. If you input a series of thoughts or commands, you can run a mental program. Most mental inconsistency occurs when the thought process centers on what the environment is giving it instead of something pre-programmed by you in advance. If you do not have a consistent picture in the Conscious Mind each time, you cannot hope to duplicate the necessary subconscious skill.

It is possible to duplicate an exact mental series of pictures before every performance, thereby achieving mental consistency. Let's look at a golf example. A player will have a specific mental program for a putt, but it will not necessarily be the same mental program that they would use for a tee shot. Most players will have two distinct mental programs. One for putting and one used for full swing shots. For some, they will stick to one mental program. The key is to keep it consistent for like shots.

The mental program is a series of thoughts, that, when pictured, will trigger the Subconscious to perform the appropriate action. This mental program controls the thought process occupying the Conscious Mind. An occupied Conscious Mind cannot pressure out, choke, or have a break in concentration.

The mental program should be run every time for every golf shot. The program will vary from one player to another. We work with hundreds of golfers and none of them have the exact same mental program however, they all follow the required guidelines and format.

Before considering the format of the mental program we must first look into the criteria of a mental program. The mental program should meet the following criteria. If one of these criteria is not met then the player will not have mental consistency.

First, the mental program must occupy the Conscious Mind. The thought process must give the Conscious Mind something to do to stay active, but not in a complex way. We want thoughts that will aid us in hitting the shot we desire. For most situations this thought process should be something unrelated to the swing. The main purpose of the mental program is to aid the player in hitting the ball subconsciously. If the player is active-minded just prior to hitting the ball it may disrupt a subconscious shot.

Second, the mental program must transfer power to the Subconscious Mind. We want to hit the ball subconsciously; therefore we want our conscious thought process to end when the swing is initiated. If we think about performing and executing the movements required to hit the shot during the actual swing, it is difficult to hit the ball subconsciously. Think about tying your shoe. Remember the first time you tried this as a kid? You thought about all of the things you needed to do in a certain order. If you messed up any of the steps your shoelace would come undone, but once you got to the point of tying the shoe without thinking of the steps you could tie your shoe without conscious effort. The process became subconscious. The thought process in the mental program should increase the probability of hitting the ball subconsciously.

Third, it must be duplicable. If you can't duplicate this thought process you will never have mental consistency. The goal for the mental program is to act

81

like a switch, moving you from conscious thought to subconscious action. This cannot be accomplished if you vary your thought process before the action. We want the same thought process in the mental program for every shot. When we change what we picture, the body responds differently and the shot goes offline.

To help aid in this matter, try keeping it simple. The simpler, the better, this is the fourth criteria. The mental program you use should be something that is easy to do and easy to remember. If it is hard to duplicate, you won't be able to have the mental consistency needed to perform at your top level of subconscious ability.

Finally, the mental program is player specific. I have worked with thousands of athletes in all types of sports. I can tell you that every one of them uses a different mental program. We suggest that the performer determine their mental program as long as it meets the criteria. Use the examples at the end of the chapter as a guideline.

The Breakdown of the Mental Program

The mental program should be run every time for every similar golf shot. The program we teach normally has three or four main steps or points. Your style of play and length of your pre-shot routine will dictate the length of your mental program. Let's take a look at the different steps.

The Point of Initiation
The Point of Alignment
The Point of Direction
The Point of Focus

The Point of Initiation

This is the starting point of the program. It must have a physical cue. The physical cue helps bring focus to the task at hand. This will vary from player to player, but some examples are taking a deep breath, gripping the club, tightening the glove, stepping into the shot or tapping the club head on the ground. It doesn't matter what you use, as long as the point of initiation is consistent. The purpose of this step is to provide a clear start point that allows the player to narrow their focus as they move into the shot.

The Point of Alignment

Most players think about aligning themselves to the target in this step.

The Point of Direction

Next, shift your concentration to what it looks like to get the shot you want. This step is important because it brings focus to the action you want to take.

We want to narrow our focus and move toward the shot. This step occurs when the player looks at the chosen target. It is the middle part of the mental program and it brings the player into the focus point of what they want to have happen and therefore reducing any negative thoughts into the Conscious Mind.

This step is important, because it is the transition point from what we want to do, to actually doing it. We must narrow the focus toward the target.

The Point of Focus

The point of focus is the last thing you picture before you take action, in this case hitting the ball. It is the end of the mental program. This is the most critical part of the mental program because it sets up the action. The last thought before you take action must be something that you can duplicate as well as being something that holds your focus, keeping negative thoughts out. The main purpose for the point of focus is to reduce any negative thoughts that can occur before the player hits the ball. The last thing a player needs is to have a negative thought right before they hit the shot. After the point of focus the player initiates the swing and is in the action phase of the golf shot.

The following are examples of a mental program for golf. Remember that these are only examples. You should explore different mental programs and see which one works for you the best. Once you have decided on the type of mental program you want, you need to personalize the steps to make it your own. A three step mental program is commonly used in putting. The player is over the ball and aligned with the target and has taken a few practice strokes with the putter.

Three Step Mental Program

Point of Initiation: Place the putter on the ground, aligned with the ball.

Point of Direction: The player takes a last look at his target and mentally rehearses the shot he wants to hit.

Point of Focus: Bring focus back to the ball and run your mental phrase. Example: Say to yourself "one...two...three."

Four Step Mental Program

In the following example the player is behind the ball and starts the mental program before they step into the shot. This example might be used by players in a full swing shot.

Point of Initiation: Line up behind the ball so that you are standing in a direct line with the ball and the target. The physical trigger might be stepping out with your left foot as you go toward the set up.

Point of Alignment: Think about aligning with the target and attaining proper posture for the shot.

Point of Direction: Look at the target and mentally rehearse the ball flight toward the target area.

Point of Focus: Bring focus back to the ball and run your mental phrase. Example: "Execute."

Keys to Remember

When running a mental program you must keep the Conscious Mind occupied. The thoughts you use during this time can be anything, as long as it aids in good performance and it is not negative. This thought process does not have to be related to the action at hand. We have seen many players use different versions of mental programs. Most players will use thoughts or words during this period, but some will use images or focus on breathing. The following are some examples of the different types of mental programs that are used during the point of focus.

Phrase related to golf: "See the line, feel the stroke." Jim uses this mental program to help him stay focused before he putts. This keeps him focused on what he wants to accomplish, but not on the outcome. It also reduces any chances of negative thoughts creeping into his mind.

Phrase not related to golf: "I love green grass." Caney uses this mental program because she already has the ability to make the putt, she just wants to get her mind out of the way and focus on something unrelated to the action. Her focus point is on the blade of grass and the back edge of the ball; therefore this mental routine works very well in her point of focus.

Breathing: Cameron doesn't like to use thoughts because it causes him to over think the shot. He has decided to focus on his breathing right before he hits the ball. This works well for players who are active-minded.

Using Imagery: John is a player that finds it hard to use phrases or focus on breathing. Being a painter has helped John come up with a unique way of staying focused. To occupy the Conscious Mind in a way to allow the action to happen automatically, John visualizes a sea scene with the ocean wave coming onto the beach. When the water retreats back into the ocean, John starts his swing. The mental image of the water on the beach moving back is his trigger for the club head to move. The end result is John is able to hit the ball subconsciously.

Song Lyric: Some players find it easier to sing a short song lyric at a point of focus. It can help with rhythm and tempo. For some this can be a distraction. The main thing is to come up with something that works specifically for you.

It is important to have mental consistency throughout your play. If you use a phrase that is related to golf it must be the same phrase used with every golf swing. The same holds true with images. Top performers are able to duplicate this mental program. You must find something that you can duplicate that will hold your focus.

Mental Program for Rifle Shooting

Here is the mental program I ran for the standing position. It has five steps:

The Point of Initiation
The Point of Attitude
The Point of Direction
The Point of Control
The Point of Focus

The Point of Initiation: This is the starting point of the program. In rifle shooting, the point of initiation is loading the rifle. Prior to loading, the shooter can think about almost anything as long as it is not negative. However, counting your score while shooting is always considered an error. The point of initiation may vary from person to person. Some may choose picking up the rifle as the start point. Others may start the mental program after scoping the previous shot is accomplished. It does not matter as long as the point of initiation is consistent.

The Point of Attitude: Once the rifle is loaded, the shooter pictures what it feels like to shoot a ten. Picture the feeling of success. See the bullet hole in the center of the ten ring. How does it feel to perform at your best? As you experience this feeling, your Subconscious moves you to get the ten.

The Point of Direction: Next, shift your concentration to what it looks like to get the ten. In this step, you rehearse getting a ten. You imagine proper sight alignment. You imagine the rifle fires. You have a proper follow-through, and a ten is the result.

The Point of Control: When shooting outside you should make one quick look at the wind flags to see if the wind has changed in speed or direction. Then, you center concentration on the most critical part of your action. In rifle shooting, the point of control is to make the hold slow and small. Think slower, smaller, slower, smaller.

The Point of Focus: The point of focus is the last thing you picture before you fire the shot and end the mental program. My point of focus is centering the target in the front sight.

Every sport or performance will have its unique way of using this tool. All mental programs will have at least three steps regardless of application: Point of Initiation, Point of Direction and Point of Focus. Some applications might require adding additional steps such as Point of Alignment or Point of Control. The key point here is to determine in advance what you are going to think about just prior to the action in your sport. What thoughts meet the criteria that I have given you? Running a mental program gives you control instead of giving up control to your environment. Once you master the mental program you have gained an important advantage over your competition.

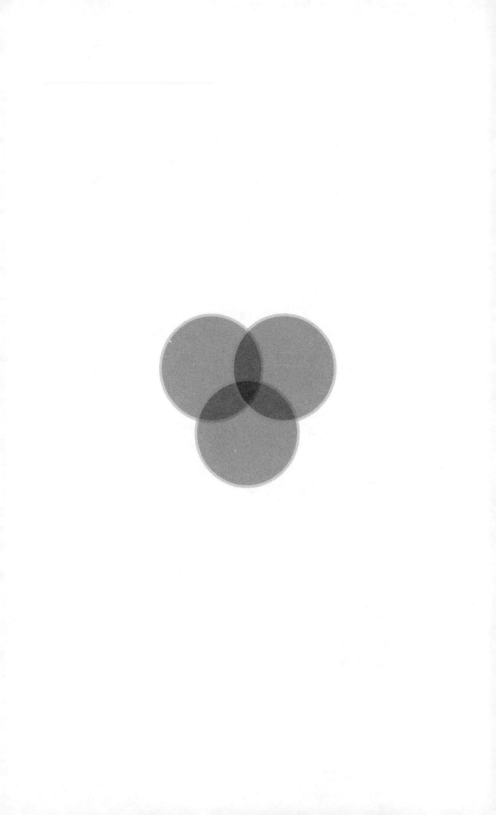

Chapter 9
Pressure - Is It Friend or Foe?

How can I avoid the pressure that I feel when competing? This question or something like it comes up a lot from our clients. In fact, I might have asked that same question early in my career. We are conditioned by the commonly held idea that pressure is a bad thing. If it's bad, then we need to avoid it.

That idea presented a problem for me because every time I competed in a big competition I felt pressure. I didn't feel pressure in training very often. Interestingly enough, it did not seem to cause my scores to go down but it presented me with concern and caused increased anxiety when it occurred. In my more than fifty years as both a competitor and a coach I have known only a few athletes that say that they do not feel something different in competition. For many, the effects of pressure are so destructive that they cause loss of points at critical times at best and the premature termination of careers at worst. However, many elite athletes find that the pressure of competition is useful, even essential, to the attainment of their best performances.

You should not want or need to avoid pressure.

"Pressure, is not something you need to avoid. It is something you need to use."

The first thing we must do to control a thing is to understand a thing. The negative effects of pressure seem to be more prevalent in players that have trouble winning. You can hear competitors talking about butterflies, being tight and the infamous choke. We seem to have a great vocabulary for the dark side of pressure and few words for the good side. The good side of pressure just doesn't make it as topic of conversation in a negatively charged world, but it should. Pressure, simply put, is neither positive nor negative. Pressure is like air. Too much and you have a hurricane. Too little and you suffocate. But in the correct amount it is the breath of life.

Fact is we need pressure. Half the fun of competing would be gone without it. We just need it in the right amount. I've spent years trying to understand the phenomenon so I can use it to my advantage. Here's what I've come up with. Pressure is two things at the same time: anxiety and tension.

Anxiety

Anxiety is fear. It is almost always viewed as a negative but think about it. Fear is what keeps you from driving too fast, following too close to the car in front of you and paying that credit card bill on

time. Fear in a competition, however, can be paralyz-
ing. We can be afraid of not doing well which usually
means that we will not be happy and we will have
a long ride home. Bummer. Here is the good news,
fear is overcome by experience. I've got to admit I
was scared in my first big competition but the fear
dropped with exposure to pressure situations.

Someone once said that the final in the Olympics is the greatest pressure situation a person can
face short of a loss of life encounter. I might add that
pressure also increases in direct proportion to your
chances of winning. I've been there, and I agree.
When I won my Olympic Gold in Montreal I was the
favorite and I felt the pressure but I did not feel fear.
I did feel tension.

Tension

That is the other side of pressure. Tension is your
level of excitement. Everything we do best has a corresponding level of tension. If we are too relaxed we
might lose focus. If we are too nervous we might
rush the process or over-try. People have a natural
tension state. Some are calm by nature while others
are bouncing off of the walls most of the time. Sports
also have different natural tension states. Sports like
fencing, boxing, tennis and downhill skiing are high
excitement sports. These athletes are pumped and
full of adrenalin from the start. Adrenalin increases

the pulse rate and moves the tension level up, way up. However, again this is not all bad. An adrenalin push can cause increased endurance, added strength and increased awareness of the senses. Archery and golf are low tension sports while International Rifle is just above coma. Shotgun sports and long distance running tend toward being medium in excitement level. So, if you are a naturally high excitement person in a low excitement sport you may have more trouble with tension control than someone more naturally balanced to their sport. If that is the case some proven excitement control techniques must be learned, practiced and mastered.

If you are too nervous in a competition I have three suggestions that can help to match your excitement level to your sport.

Recognize that pressure is positive and something that you can control.

First, pressure is not in your imagination. It is real, a good thing and you can use it to your advantage. You must accept that it is normal to feel something in a pressure situation. This is your body saying, "This is important. Pay attention." Accept the advantages of stress and expect that your scores will be better for having felt pressure. Also do not be surprised if you occasionally do not notice pressure's effects even in a big competition. Pressure does not always make itself known to the Conscious Mind.

Focus on what you want to see happen, not on what is stressing you.

Most of the time when competitors experience point-reducing tension levels it's because they are thinking about something that causes the level to rise. "Boy, I really need this one!" "What am I doing wrong?" "If I finish this hole with a birdie I win the tournament." These thoughts are on outcomes, not on the process of performing. Thinking about what you are doing wrong or counting your score just increases the negative effects of stress. Keep your mind on the process of doing well and the outcome will take care of itself.

Use a planned, practiced recovery strategy.

Sometimes the pressure seems to increase just after a poor shot, and you might need a way to recover. One effective technique is to have a planned and trained recovery strategy. All recovery strategies have two important things in common. First you must get your mind off of the things that are increasing the tension/anxiety response. Secondly, you must do something that you can absolutely control. Here is an example. You've had a bad series of shots, you begin to think about your score and you need to recover. First, concentrate on your breathing. Breathe in a practiced pattern for say three breaths. Then relax a specific muscle group such as your neck and shoulders. Finally, visualize being in complete control of a good performance. You can only think of one thing at a time so while you are thinking about these things you cannot be still thinking negatively. Also, you can 100 percent control your method of breathing, the relaxation of your muscles and the visualization so the second step is accomplished as well. Now, when you refocus on your next series you should be recovered and should perform well.

An additional recommendation might seem strange but this really works. If you catch yourself becoming a bit nervous and need a quick tool to get you calmed down try yawning. That's right. FAKE a YAWN. The same chemicals that cause your muscles to relax when you yawn naturally also seem to work just the same when you fake a yawn. Next time you watch the Olympics on TV watch for this technique. You will see someone in a pressure situation yawning. Everyone else will think he is really in control. You will know the truth. He might be using the fake yawn to control unwanted tension.

Remember coal under pressure produces a diamond. Competitors in control under pressure produce winning scores.

Chapter 10
The Number One Mental Problem

Frustrated, a competitor says, "I've got a problem, and I know it is mental. It just has to be because I can hit every shot on the course in practice and when I get in the big competition I make too many bad shots. I miss a lot of easy putts, and I just don't know what to do. Now don't get me wrong. I can take being beaten by a better player, but I just can't stand beating myself. What am I doing wrong and how do I fix it?"

Every week our phone rings with this kind of person on the other end of the phone line. He did not want to make this call. He has tried everything he knows to fix this problem but to no avail. This guy is a serious competitor that has made a big investment of time and money in his sport and wants to do well. He has good equipment and has taken training from some of the best coaches on the planet. So, why is he so frustrated? He could be a victim of what I believe is the number one mental problem among competitors…..Over-Trying.

When I began shooting I believed that to do your best at a sport you should give it 110 percent. That's what I'd always heard, and I had done that in PE class. I ran as fast as I could in the 100 yard dash. I was not fast but I gave it all I had. I accepted the fact that to try hard was to do well, and if I gave an activity less than my all, I deserved to lose. Now trying your hardest may be the best thing to do in push-ups or to win a 100 yard dash, but there are many activities that do not work well when you give them your all.

It seems to me that all things in life require a certain amount of mental effort to do them well. If we give them one percent less effort than is required or one percent more than is needed, the performance tends to drop. The key is to find the proper level of mental effort for the task. Some sports tend to require a lot of power. The greater the power expended, the greater the chance of winning. These high-power sports require certain muscle groups to be tensed to the maximum. That is not always the case. We work with a lot of shotgun shooters so let's look at a shotgun example. Shotgun shooting requires a light hand on the gun and fluid motion. We are rarely moving the gun as fast as possible. Shooting requires control, not power and when we try to over-power the gun we tend to lose control. Shooters tend to experience a greater chance of over-powering the gun when they are TRYING to make a shot on a target instead of TRUSTING that the shot will subconsciously come together. This is a prime example of over-trying. We might even hear ourselves think, "I HAVE to hit these targets." When you push yourself you tend to tense up. The result is a missed target.

So, what are we to do? Is it possible to find the effort point where we are trying just hard enough and not exceed this amount? I believe that it is possible but it is not an easy task. I believe that 95 percent of the competitors in a competition are over-trying at least some of the time and many are over-trying in the entire competition. Why? I'll give you three reasons why competitors over-try.

First, they are afraid to trust their subconscious skill. Many competitors do not practice enough to really know what their subconscious skill level is. They try to compensate for this at the competition by being "extra careful". EXTRA CAREFUL = OVER-TRYING. Many competitors work hard enough in training but still work extra hard in the competition. WORKING HARD IN COMPETITION = OVER-TRYING. Champions work hard in training and work easy in the competition. The key is to work hard enough in practice to just trust your Subconscious in the competition.

Second, they are thinking about outcome instead of process. If you are worried about your score, your competition, your last failure or anything other than the process of executing, you are thinking about outcome instead of process. You cannot think about two things at the same time so your focus is pulled away from execution and toward outcome. When this happens we almost always over-try to make the action happen instead of just letting it happen.

Thinking about outcome = Over-trying

Finally, most performers over-try because they operate on the misconception that trying harder will produce a greater chance of success. Is this really true? Think about the times you have recorded your best scores. Include training and competition. How hard were you trying? I work with many of the top technical instructors in the USA and they have reported to me that many times they do their best performing when demonstrating how to execute a task to their students. They perform well with ease because they are not trying to win a competition, they are just demonstrating the process. They are not working hard. They are hardly working. So try dialing it back a little in a competition. Let it happen and see what happens.

Sometimes players play really well when they do not particularly care if they do well or not. If this competition is not really an important one or they are just out to enjoy the day the pressure is off and scores reflect it. If your performance in competition drops compared to training then you are most likely over-trying. A logical solution might be to care less in the competition, saying, "It is not important how I do." I do not like this solution. Caring less will make you careless which is the opposite end of the same mental error. I suggest you change what you care about. Stop caring so much about score, your competition and winning, and care more about executing your process. Focus on the next step not on the final result. Your job in a competition is to execute the process of performing not on anything else. Your job in training is to isolate and master the steps of performing well. If you successfully execute these steps in a competition your score and winning will take care of themselves.

Finally, I encourage you to have fun in competitions. The optimum mental level and let's just have fun today are really close together. We spend a lot of time and money on sport and it should be fun to come together and compete. If we stay focused on process and try just hard enough, the chance that we will see our name higher on the leader board is improved.

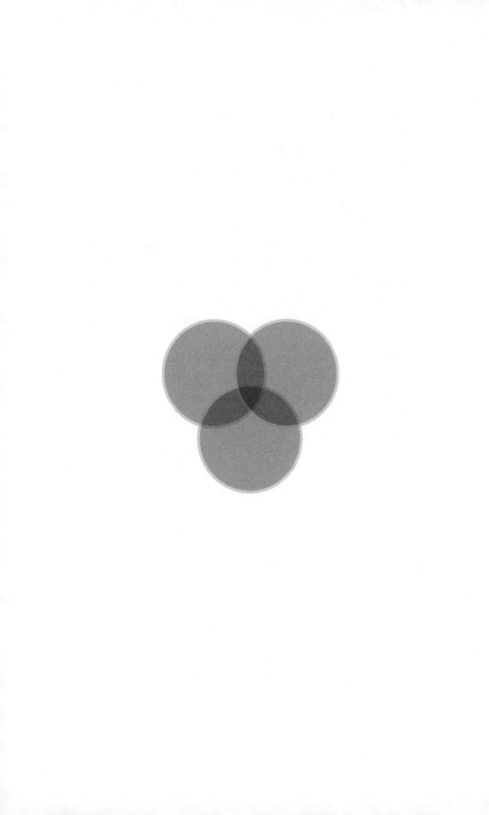

Section 3

Building the
Subconscious Circle

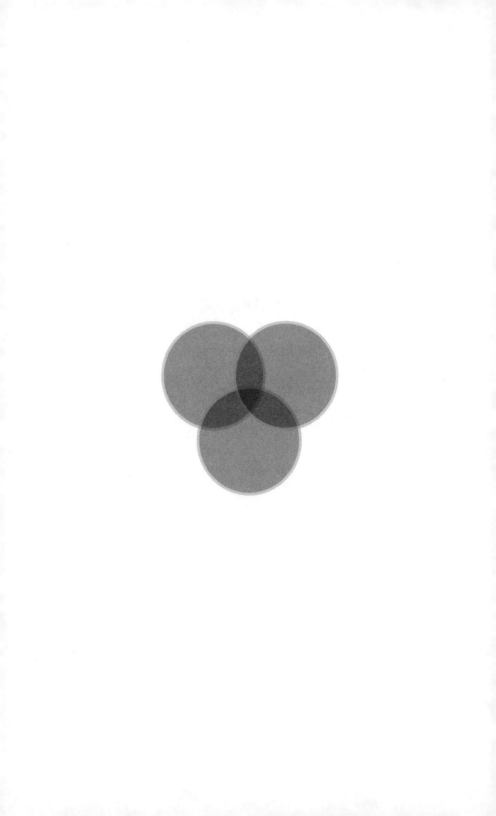

Chapter 11
The Skills Factory

Every year we see skilled athletes that make performing well look easy. Some of them are as young as ten years of age. This usually generates a lot of buzz and we often hear comments like, "He is going to go far, look how talented he is." This happens all over the world, but the reality is that talent has little to do with it. I recognize that there is something different about the five percent of the people that accomplish 95 percent of the winning but it cannot be explained away so easily as calling it talent. People use the word as if to suggest that the players that dominate are somehow gifted by God and that explains why they are so successful. They just have a talent for it. You either have it or you don't. End of discussion.

I have been guilty of using the word talent as a synonym for the word skilled. This is not an issue most of the time, but it becomes problematic when you confuse acquired skill with skills that one is born with. If you are 7' 6" tall, coordinated and fast, you have a natural advantage in basketball over someone 5' 2" tall. I'll grant you that, but great players are not created; they create themselves.

To be successful you must look at those who have made it to the top. For many inspiring competitors who compete at a young age, making it to world level is a goal of theirs. Certainly all of the players who make it to the elite levels are skilled, but the world is full of skilled players that are not successful. What makes the difference?

I don't think I have a natural ability for shooting. In fact, I am still searching for my special talent. But I have known athletes who seem to have a passion for their sport. One such shooter is Soma Dutta from India.

I met Soma for the first time in 1982. Her family, eager to find an international shooting coach, accompanied her to my International Shooting School in Seguin, Texas to check me out. Soma stayed at the academy for one month while we evaluated each other. At the young age of 14, this resident of Calcutta held every major national record in her country. Her records for women and juniors exceeded the best results recorded by men as well.

Passionate is the only word I know to describe this incredible young athlete. Just as a great artist seems to lose track of time when working on a masterpiece, Soma possessed a special passion for training. Most shooters tire of training after four to five hours. If I would have allowed it, she would have spent ten. I would insist she take a day off, and then find her sneaking up to the range to shoot.

Soma returned to the school the next year for several months. She shot in the Olympics in 1984 at the age of sixteen, the youngest shooter on the line. She was ranked second in Asia and among the top twenty in the world. She won a coveted quota slot in 1986, awarded to fewer than forty shooters in the world, qualifying her to compete in the 1988 Olympic Games in Seoul. The advantage the passionate athlete possesses is difficult to measure. Obviously, all skilled competitors work hard. Though it is difficult to compare myself to Soma, I believe we share one thing in common, a passion for the process. I cannot explain why I arrived at the range before my peers and was often the last one to leave. Shooting was never something I HAD to do. If you wish to say that passion is a gift from God, I will not disagree with you. It appears that the number of people that have a real passion to practice is much less than the ones that are made to train.

The elite also seem to have an uncommon persistence that defies explanation. When the going gets tough the tough get going may be trite but it is true. I believe that adversity creates a special form of motivation in people. I sincerely believe that if I had been an average baseball player I would not have won an Olympic gold medal in shooting. I was so frustrated at being a poor player that I had a special motivation to succeed. Perhaps this explains in part why I was so driven to train. One thing is certain; training produces skill.

Skill is developed in the Subconscious Mind. The amount of skill and the size of the Subconscious circle are determined by the quality of the training, the quantity of the training, and the efficiency of this training.

Quality is a function of both the value of the knowledge you are exposed to and the efficacy of the instructors that present it to you. Is the information you are presented with the best available? Is it up to date? Is it well presented? Are you learning from books, CDs, videos or personalized instruction? How skilled are the instructors or authors at presenting the information? These are the factors that affect the quality of your training; the better the quality the better the training effect.

Quantity is the amount of time you actually spend in learning and growing. It is not always directly related to the amount of time spent at the activity. It's possible to be at a training session and do many things other than learn and grow. It is not always a function of how many attempts you make. Half-hearted attempts are ineffective and dilute the training process.

Efficiency is directly related to how balanced a player becomes in training all three mental processes at the same time in the training session. If a player is thinking things that maximize performance, the Conscious Mind is built. If he is utilizing proper technique, the Subconscious Mind is enhanced. If he is picturing what he wants to have happen and carefully avoids negative imprints, the Self-Image grows as well. When all three of these things happen simultaneously the training is very efficient. If, however, the player's conscious thoughts are not those that maximize a good performance or he beats himself up after a bad shot, the training becomes less efficient, even if proper technique is used. If any of the mental processes are ignored or performed poorly the efficiency of the training session is negatively affected.

Guidelines

To better understand training, we will look at 7 guidelines to building Subconscious skills.

Training Guideline Number 1

Catch yourself doing something right.

All too often, I hear the comment, "What am I doing wrong? If I could only isolate my problem areas and find the cause of my failures, I could be a success." Nothing could be further from the truth. That's like saying if you study all the wrong ways of doing a math problem, you will learn how to do it right. What you really need to do is study one or two ways of doing something right instead of a hundred ways to do it wrong. If you study failure, you will become an expert in how to fail. So, stop catching yourself doing things wrong and trying to find out why you are failing. Focusing on success alone builds Self-Image. Here is an example. A golfer hits a good shot and says, "Well, I guess I just got lucky that time." When he hits a bad shot he says, "Why do I always do that?" His Self-Image shrinks every time he repeats this kind of behavior. A better solution would be to say, "What do I need to do to make that shot good?" if it is not good or "That's a good shot. What did I do right?" if it is a good one. See the difference? This may sound so basic and common sense to you but how many times do we see accomplished veterans making this mistake?

Training Guideline Number 2

Train four or five days a week.

The information in this guideline is applicable only to performers while developing skill. It is not uncommon for performers that have acquired skill to train little or none at all and do very well in competition. The best athletes in the world had to go through a development period. Few train the same today as when they were acquiring skill. You cannot become skilled if you do not train regularly. The question to answer is: How much is too much and how much is not enough? For most activities, during your development period, you will burn out if you do them seven days a week. If you train less than four days a week, you will not maximize your development. If you train only one day a week, it is probable that you will deteriorate faster than if you do not train at all. That's right, one day a week is worse than no training at all. If you train two or three days a week, you can maintain your level, but you may not improve. Therefore, training four to six days a week is optimal to move up the mastery curve. You may not be able to sustain this during heavy competition-driven periods so maximize this guideline in the off-season if you can. Golf and Shooting can be year-round sports but you will benefit greatly in scheduling periods of intense training.

Training Guideline Number 3

Wherever you are, be all there.

When you go from the office to the golf course, leave the office thoughts in the office. When you go home to the family, leave the bad golf round at the course. When you go from home to the office, leave the home problems at home. Wherever you are, be there 100 percent. This may be the most important training guideline in this chapter. When we carry problems from one area of life into another, focus is lost in the primary area. This is why this guideline is so important.

A person must have the discipline to stay focused on the task at hand. If the task is a business call, you cannot effectively handle it when thinking of something that went wrong at home. Worry about that problem when you can do something about it. If you scheduled practice from 1:00 PM to 3:00 PM, you should do just that practice during those two hours. There is nothing wrong with catching up on things with friends, but do not let it interfere with your training.

Training Guideline Number 4

Rehearse the match day often within the training session.

Treat training days as if they had the same importance as the most crucial competition day. At some point in every day take some time to imagine that you are in competition and playing well. Be vivid in your rehearsal, see it, hear it, taste it, smell it, and feel it. Another common time to perform this rehearsal is the night before a competition. Tournament days can be stressful and PGA Tour players tell us that they prepare for success by mentally playing the round in their mind the night before the competition. It is extremely important to birdie hole after hole. This form of practice helps set up the Self-Image for a successful tournament day.

Training Guideline Number 5

When you are playing well, play a lot.

This is an expression I borrowed from my teammate in the Olympics, Jack Writer. It applies to all performers in the same manner as it does in shooting. I remember one day Jack and I were training together. I asked him what he was going to shoot that day.

"I will shoot 50 shots in the standing position and 100 shots in kneeling," he said.

"I will do the same thing," I said.

We both started shooting standing. Soon I finished my 50 shots and started kneeling. Jack continued in standing. After I finished my 100 shots kneeling, Jack was still shooting standing. I went to lunch. When I returned, Jack was still shooting standing. Finally he finished. I asked him why he changed his mind and shot so much standing. That's when he told me, "I was shooting above my personal record. When I do that I always keep shooting. When you are shooting well, shoot a lot."

The best time to practice your drives on the driving range is right after you have crushed some good ones. Keep hitting the driver. If you're on a roll, keep on going. This helps to reinforce the good experience you are having and therefore make it more likely to occur in the future. Likewise, if you are slicing badly, now is not the time to hit another bucket of balls. If you are having a bad day, stop training. Do not practice losing.

Training Guideline Number 6

We raise ourselves to the standard we are around.

Train with people who are better than you, and you will get better. When you train with people who are not in your league, you tend play just like them. This is why schools, like Jim McLean Golf Academy in Fort Worth, are good places to train. It is not uncommon for juniors to be on the putting green with PGA Tour players. Veteran players are helpful to the young ones coming into the sport and this form of sportsmanship is common in the academy environment and in the golf culture in general. This practice is not exclusive to golf, and we often see champions in all sports sharing with young athletes.

Another advantage to playing in environments like this is that we can learn from others, by watching their play. We can see how they handle certain situations that might be useful in your game. The Self-Image benefits from the imprints of better technique that the player receives by watching skilled players. If this is true then do we lower ourselves by playing with players that are worse than us? Frankly, I doubt it, and I will give you two reasons why. First, I've had the honor to train World Skeet Champion Todd Bender for many years. Todd is recognized as one of the top instructors in skeet in the world and trains hundreds of shooters every year. Todd sees a lot of error but rarely makes an error when competing. Why? I believe that his Self-Image is able to separate who he is from his students. There is just not enough relationship there to cause the imprint of a student missing a target to affect Todd's shooting. I experienced a similar situation when I ran the International Shooting School in Seguin, Texas in the 1980s. I was shooting at the top of my game and teaching and watching shooters of lesser skill every day.

Secondly, we tend to be more affected by the behavior of people that are where we want to go than by those that are where we have been. Perhaps this is because we do not goal set to go backward. One thing is certain, however; we are greatly affected by people that are at the same level as ourselves and by the thoughts and statements we make about our own performances. So, I encourage you to become someone that helps others and have no fear that it will damage your performance in the future.

Training Guideline Number 7

Plan your year.

Begin by determining the competition schedule for the year. In most sports, there are several big meets scheduled for the year, culminating in the nationals. Schedule these events on your master calendar in your journal.

Next, count the number of training days you have available to you until the next competition. Now count the days available for the entire year. You may be surprised just how few there are.

Look for possible conflicts with your attendance at these special events. College students may not be able to move their finals to go to a match, but they might be able to register for classes that allow them to have Fridays free as travel days. Try to maximize the hours you have available by planning in advance. Planning in advance reduces the loss of training days due to running out of supplies, such as targets or ammunition.

Next, you should file a training budget. If you are fortunate, you have a coach or manager who can help you with this step. A training budget has projections for at least four areas: equipment, travel, fees, and supplies.

What new equipment will you need to reach your goals for the year? What is your plan to acquire them and when is the best time to make purchases?

What are the travel costs to get to matches, sessions with instructors, or training sessions? By planning in advance, you may be able to save on advance purchases for air fare or combine two competitions into one trip.

What fees will be charged for entering competitions, national association memberships, seminars, and coaching?

What supplies will you use? Include ammunition, targets, and cleaning supplies. Avoid the possibility of lost training days by scheduling advance purchases of these essential items.

You divide your year into quarterly sessions. The lengths of the quarters are individual and sport-specific. During the first quarter of a training year, after you have just finished a needed rest from last season's competitions, evaluate your performance. During this session, you should establish your training plan, make out your budget, and set your schedule for the next year. Evaluate any equipment or technique changes you plan to make in the coming competitive year. Now is the time to test new ideas. Order new equipment, evaluate it, and make improvements during this session. Later in the competition phase, you will not want to change things.

During the second quarter, concentrate on conditioning. In this quarter, you work especially hard on drills that will strengthen you for the demanding seasons ahead. Shooting is not a seasonal sport. We shoot major competitions year round. If your sport is not seasonal, you may have to compete within the conditioning session. If so, understand that your competition has the same challenge. It was always motivating to me to shoot against my major competitors in the winter season. If I seemed behind, I worked harder. If I was ahead, I worked even harder because I knew that the competition would be trying to catch me.

During the third quarter, you are ready for competition. During this period, you will be attending major competitions leading up to your national championship. By this time, you should be properly conditioned and at your best. The focus in this session is peak performance. Training centers on match simulations rather than drills. Avoid experimentation with new equipment and techniques.

During the fourth quarter, rest and reflect on how the season progressed. You have done your best in the nationals. It is a time for much needed rest, repair, and reflection. Do not make the mistake of omitting this step. You may think you can get a jump on your competition by training at this time, but chances are you will weaken yourself in the long run. Also, you need the time away from your sport to reflect on your goals, training methods, and concepts. It is during this period that you establish an outline for your training during the year.

Finally, you should set up training objectives for the year in three major areas. First, determine what objectives you want to meet in training by the end of each quarter session. Second, determine how many hours you will average in each training day. Third, plan how you will spend those hours. By following these guidelines, you can develop a well-planned training program that should improve your results in competition.

Chapter 12
Performance Analysis

Most of us take a lesson from a coach at some time in our life, and we are all self-coached every day. Has this ever happened to you? Your coach asks you "How have you been doing?" and you say something like "OK, I guess." You say that because you cannot with precision remember what you have been doing because you have no record of it. I believe that the primary reason people do not keep a record in a Performance Journal is that they have never been given a really good reason to do it and because they have never been taught how to do it.

OK. Here is why you MUST record your progress in a Performance Journal. I'll give you three reasons. First, you cannot manage what you do not measure. Simply put, you cannot afford to be in the dark concerning your progress. You need to have a plan to reach your goals. So, you set a goal, make a plan and go to a competition. Let's say you do not reach your goal at that competition. If you have a well-documented Performance Journal you can easily determine if your plan failed or you just failed to work your plan. Winning is not an accident. You must plan your work, work your plan and be accountable.

Secondly, I will not coach an individual without a Performance Journal and if you are a coach you should demand it of your performers. Why? Because without one you are wasting a lot of time when you try to coach someone. I know, by referring to the Performance Journal of my performers, how often they are practicing, how long the practice lasts, what went on in the training session or competition, what worked and what did not work, what the objective of each session was and if it was accomplished. I know what equipment was used, when a change in equipment occurred and the reason for the change. I know what the competition results were, what the weather was like on the field and the start time of the event. And what is even more important is that if I can determine this level of information from the journal then the performer can as well. How does a coach know this amount of detail if someone does not record it? I am not willing to trust my memory or that of the student on these critical issues. No journal, no coaching from me. You can't manage what you don't measure.

Finally, if you are using the journal only to record information you are not maximizing the use of a Performance Journal. I believe that the primary benefit of a Performance Journal is to build Self-Image by imprinting both real and rehearsed images. Every time we think about something it imprints and shapes our Self-Image. I believe that when we talk about something it imprints with greater power than just thinking about it. Talking about a bad performance is a fine way to cause it to become a habit. We become what we think and talk about. Mental images that are written down have a greater impact on the Self-Image than those that we simply talk about. If you really want to change your Self-Image make a habit of writing down what you wish to have happen. You tend to become what you write about. But, be careful, do not write about anything that you do not want to have happen.

So, if keeping a Performance Journal is such a good idea why do so few people take the time to keep one. Again I'll give you three reasons. First, they keep a diary not a journal. My definition of a diary is to record your impressions, good and bad, of what happened today. Recording the statistics can be helpful and we will do this as well in a Performance Journal but if you record your mistakes you are making a huge mental error and the Self-Image suffers. Let's say you have a bad day at the event and you record all of your bad shots and just how you performed them. The principle of reinforcement works against you big time. You have just improved your chance of shooting these shots again in the future by writing them down in your diary. A Performance Journal, by my definition, has no references to bad shots, bad experiences or poor performances. It is a Performance Journal not a lack of Performance Journal. People who keep diaries often find their performance suffers in the future. When this happens they do the correct thing. They throw the diary away. Diaries don't work but Performance Journals do and are essential if you really want to improve your performance in competitions.

Secondly, performers do not know how to keep a Performance Journal and are rarely taught to do so by those who coach them. If they are taught anything they are taught to keep a diary and we have already covered that issue. OK, so what should be in a Performance Journal? I recommend that you record critical information in a journal every day at the end of training or competition.

You should have an equipment page that is constantly updated every time you change anything. You need a competition page to record your scores in competition and an easy way to relate them to the journal pages. Keep your journal where you can record this information immediately after performing. You can remember things only so long, so do your recording before you leave the competition or training area if possible.

Finally, most people will not keep a journal because they are just lazy. Look, if you are playing just to have fun this section may not be for you but if you want to win you must separate yourself from the others in your dedication. I understand, I do not like to document things either, but I do it because not doing it is just not acceptable. It is not acceptable to be unable to remember what I have or have not done. It is not acceptable to make the same mistakes over and over because I did not record the solutions the first time. It is not acceptable to not know if my plan is correct or if it is working at all. It is not acceptable to be defeated in a shoot-off by someone keeping a Performance Journal. It is not acceptable to beat myself. It is not acceptable to lose because I'm just too lazy to do what is needed to win.

A Performance Journal will yield great benefits to you if you are a coach and have your players on the system. Both of you can track the performance because it is documented in the journal. This is a painless way to keep your players accountable to themselves and for you to keep track of what you have done for them. Ask a player who keeps a Performance Journal "How is it going?" and see if he doesn't pull out his Performance Journal and show you.

For many years I fought the concept of keeping a Performance Journal or diary. I worked hard in training, and I wanted to eliminate any superfluous activities. Still, it was not until I discovered a productive journal-keeping system that my training and match scores improved and were much more consistent. With a journal, I was able to review my progress and better evaluate my efforts using a systematic approach to record keeping. The system I created is called "Performance Analysis".

Performance Analysis is the process of recording in your Performance Journal essential information that tracks your progress. It is a complete system, taking only a few minutes a day, that utilizes positive reinforcement to build Self-Image and speed you toward your goal.

Why use a Performance Journal? A plan is not easily followed if it is not written down. It is of no use if you cannot readily refer to it. Carry it with you to all training sessions. You should use a page or two for each day, with sufficient space to enter the needed data. The purpose of the journal is to add organization to your training program, not burden you with unnecessary work.

Performance Analysis, the performance journal that we recommend and sell, is designed to do all of the things that I mentioned in this chapter and to grow your Self-Image circle at the same time. Our journal is in a durable book form that is easy to use and inexpensive to purchase. It is available on our website at www.mentalmanagementstore.com or by calling our offices at 972-899-9640.

The Elements of a Performance Journal

Our Performance Analysis Journal contains a written record of six key planning areas:

Your Competition Log
Your Equipment Log
Your General Data Section
Your Solution Analysis

Your Success Analysis
Your Daily Goal Statement

Competition and Equipment Log

This Competition Log records the competition dates, results and page numbers for the journal entries of your competitions. The Equipment Log records all the equipment you are using. You only make entries in this log when you change, add or repair equipment.

General Data Section

Fill in the date, location, event (training or competition), and the time of day and duration of the activity. Next, write down exactly what you learned and what you accomplished during this period. How many attempts did you make? How many hours did you train? How did you spend the time? What was the result or score? If you do not train or compete on a day or do anything that affects your sport or activity, do not fill out a journal page.

Three ladies are at a swimming pool. One sits in the sun, never entering the water. The second puts her feet in the water, but does not leave the pool side. The third swims twenty laps in the pool. Later, all three will say they had been swimming that day. It is easy for us to say we are training, when in fact we are spending most of our time visiting with other competitors, setting up equipment, or reflecting upon our condition, whatever it may be.

A Performance Journal entry eliminates rationalizations and just records the facts.

Solution Analysis

The Solution Analysis section is your chance to write down any solutions to challenges you have discovered during a training day. If you have a problem that you cannot find a solution for, simply state, "I'm looking for a solution to….," and then describe the problem. Also, you should write down solutions to problems you learned today in this section. Continued reference to this portion of the Performance Analysis will reduce the chance that you will repeat an error.

Success Analysis

In the Success Analysis section, write down anything you did well during a day of training. When you do this, you improve the probability that you will repeat the success. If you set a personal record, this section should be quite descriptive on that day. The journal forces you to be positive about your sport and your performance.

Goal Statement

The goal statement is the most important step of the journal page. State an objective that you intend to reach. Write it in the first person present tense, as if you have already reached it. Some examples of goals statements are:

I often shoot above 390/400.
I am on the United States Olympic team.
I often shoot below par.
I am the most consistent player on our team.

Goal statements should be achievements that are currently out of reach, but not out of sight. Every time we write down a goal, we are that much closer to its attainment. Only two things are possible. Your goal will be reached, or you will stop writing it down. As long as you continue to write down your goal statements, you are moving toward their attainment.

Performance Analysis is one of the most useful coaching tools. I learn much from reviewing a student's journal. I discover how many days a week the student is training. I know how many hours a day are spent in practice and exactly what was accomplished. I am immediately aware of the student's strengths or problem areas. I know the goals of my students and most important, so do they.

A Performance Journal provides the athlete and coach with a valuable resource for improvement,

without burdening either with unnecessary paper-
work.

Section 4

Building the
Self-Image Circle

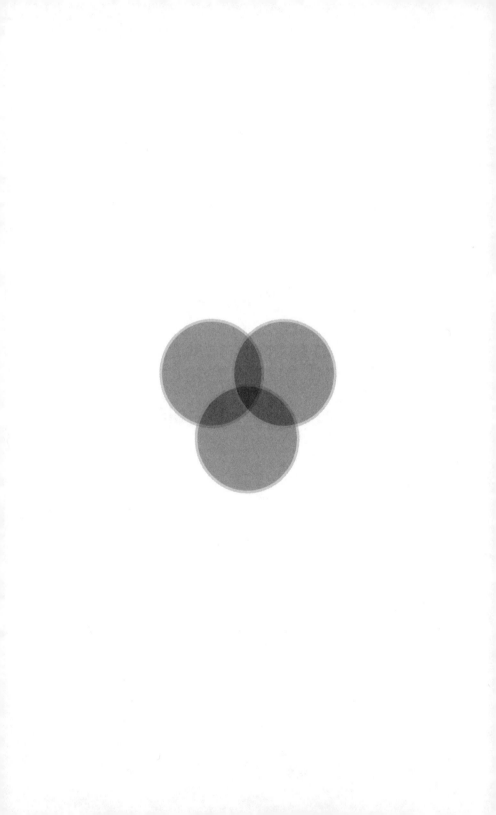

Chapter 13
Building a Better You

The Self-Image is the sum of your habits and attitudes. Your attitudes determine whether you feel positively or negatively about an item or concept. Your habits determine how you act. You will do certain things because it is consistent with your Self-Image.

Are these attitudes familiar?

I perform great in practice, but when I get in the match, my score drops.
If I do well at the beginning, I lose it at the end.
I am so busy, but I just don't seem to get much done.
I can never remember names.
I can't sell anything. I'm not that kind of person.
I could never speak before a large crowd of people.
I'm technically sound in my sport, but I choke under pressure.

These are statements I've heard from students of mine. They are all temporary Self-Image attitudes.

They can change. In fact, the same people who held these attitudes initially soon began to talk like this:

I perform better in matches than in practice.
If I start well, I finish well.
I am an efficient person who gets things done.
I'm good at remembering names.
I enjoy speaking before groups.
I'm the kind of person who people order from.
I can count on a good performance, especially under pressure.

What accounted for the change? They all experienced a change in Self-Image. When you shift the Self-Image, the change is often permanent.

We tend to perform within a certain "comfort zone". Bob bowls between 120 and 160. It is like him to bowl an occasional strike, but he has never bowled four in a row. He gets nervous when he bowls three in a row. It's not like him to hit four strikes in a row so his Self-Image executes a correction to keep him in his comfort zone; here comes an open frame. He's comfortable between 120 and 160. That's like Bob.

Your Self-Image "makes you act like you." It keeps you within your comfort zone. If you are below your zone, your Self-Image makes you uncomfortable and turns up your power until you are within the zone. Likewise, if you are above your zone, the Self-Image will cut your power, dropping you back within your zone. As long as you "act like you", the Self-Image is content and does not interfere. To change your performance, you must change your Self-Image and elevate your comfort zone.

Controlling the change in your Self-Image may be the most important skill you will ever learn. You can change any attitude you do not like. When the Self-Image changes, performance changes.

Beginners tend to have comfort zones that are quite wide with the upper and lower levels not well defined. As one improves in skill and these limits become more predictable the upper and lower limits should become closer to one another. Elite players strive for consistency in tournament scoring with very small comfort-zone variations. When your score is well below where you expect it to be in a competition, one place to look for answers is the Self-Image.

There is good news and bad news ahead. The bad news is that your performance and your Self-Image are almost always equal. If you do not like your score, there is a good chance that you need to change your Self-Image. There is more bad news. The Self-Image resists change. This is actually a good thing. If you changed too easily you would love your spouse one day and not like her/him the next. The good news is that Self-Image can change but I admit it is not easy.

The problem for most of us is that we know something has to change for our score to improve. We just do not want it to be us. We'd prefer that our problem would be solved by buying that new piece of equipment. We'd prefer that if we read another book or took another lesson we would change. We'd prefer that someone else be the problem instead of me, anything but me. But, no one can change your Self-Image for you. You have to do it yourself and the first step is to admit that you are the problem.

So, once you have decided to change, how do you do it? You can try the most common method used by frustrated players that is certain to make you even more frustrated. Just train more. That is a good way to change your Subconscious Mind but it will do little to change Self-Image. Playing more doesn't always improve Self-Image but imprinting a good performance always does.

The Self-Image you have now got that way some-how. Doesn't it make sense that you would have to change it the same way? How does Self-Image change? You change it through imprinting. Every time we hit a target we imprint a hit. This is called an actual or environmental imprint. Your environment gives you an indelible imprint every time you per-form. Let's take golf as an example. When you hit a bad shot you have just improved the chances of hitting another one in the future because your Self-Image has imprinted that it is like you to miss shots. Every time you practice or play, you risk getting a bad shot and getting a bad imprint. However, you can imagine a great shot with 100 percent accuracy. An imagined imprint is still an indelible imprint. Now, I will admit that scoring an eagle in a big competi-tion tends to have a stronger imprint than an imagined imprint but which is easier for you to do? We can imprint thousands of imagined perfect shots with 100 percent chance that they will be good ones. All it takes is a little knowledge of how to do it correctly and some effort.

My experience has been that the method of imprinting that is used affects the amount of Self-Image change. Visualization is not as effective in changing Self-Image as is rehearsal. OK, what is the difference? Most people understand visualization to mean SEEING as clearly as you can what you are actually seeing when you perform an action. I have even used the term in my work. Many players are concerned that they cannot seem to get a sharp picture and do not really SEE clearly when they try to visualize. I don't think that the clarity matters. In fact it is not what you SEE that is important but what you FEEL. Rehearse the feeling of hitting a good shot. Don't try to see it. Try to FEEL it. What does the move feel like when you do it properly? When you imprint in this way you avoid having to clearly visualize and you reinforce the non-visual aspects of the shot as well. Many good players talk about being a feel-player. When you do that you are rehearsing not visualizing.

Another factor is WHEN you rehearse. The best time to imprint is just before and just after the action of hitting the ball. Rehearse hitting a good shot both before and after the swing or putt. This causes three imprints on each shot and two of them are guaranteed to be good. Not only does this greatly improve the chance of a better score but it causes the Self-Image to grow at the same time. There is a huge cumulative effect to doing this. Can you imagine if you did this on every shot for an entire season? What an advantage. So, why do so few players do this? I believe it is because it takes extra effort and most are just are not willing to work that hard to win. That is good news as well because if you ARE willing to expend the mental energy you have an advantage on those that are not that dedicated.

Another thing to consider is that we imprint continually. The Self-Image cannot tell the difference between past, present or future events as far as imprinting is concerned. Each time you recall an experience the Self-Image imprints it again as a new event. If you think about a problem you had in the past, the Self-Image imprints it again as if it has just happened. If you imagine a future event your Self-Image imprints it as occurring now. You are in control of the imprinting process. I won the Olympics thousands of times through imprinting in the years prior to the Gold medal. Imprint anything you want to happen and you have improved your chances of actually having it happen because it becomes like you to do it.

Be careful not to think about anything that you do not wish to have happen. Do that and you imprint it as being like you. Most people worry that they will perform poorly in some part of their game. This normally intensifies just prior to a big competition. What a mistake! Keep your mind only on what you want to have happen. If you catch yourself worrying just rehearse performing well and the worries will tend to disappear.

Steps in Changing Self-Image

Changing a Self-Image that is keeping you from reaching your goals may be the most important skill you will ever learn. I believe that you can change any attitude or habit you do not want. You should experience a corresponding change in performance when the Self-Image changes. Here is how to do it in four steps.

First, you must be willing to change. Our Self-Image does not respond to the changes others want us to make. You must decide for yourself and you must choose to do it NOW.

Second, you must identify specifically the habits and/or attitudes that you need to change. Be specific. For example; "I'm looking for a solution to worrying about shooting below my average in the days just before a competition."

Third, you must identify a new Self-Image that is in direct conflict with your old one. For example, "I only think about what I want to have happen concerning up-coming competitions."

Fourth, you exchange the old Self-Image for the desired one by only imprinting the new attitude or habit and trying to eliminate imprinting the old one.

Remember, your Self-Image is the CURRENT state of YOU. It is not the FINAL state. Be aware that your Self-Image is evolving in the direction of your imprinting. The better you control your imprinting the better captain you will be of the submarine that is taking you to your goals.

Nothing is going to change unless you change. If you possessed everything that you needed to succeed, you would have reached your goal already.

As an example, Donny was a fine young basketball player who had a chance to make his school's starting squad. His defensive ability was solid. He was a good shooter, but his percentage at the free-throw line was poor. So poor in fact, that the coach hesitated to play him in critical situations. The coach knew that Donny's deficiency was a mental attitude about the free-throw line. When questioned about his not starting, Donny would say, "The coach just likes the other players better. I just don't shoot free-throws well. I never have." With that attitude, Donny had no chance to start. Also, Donny has a bad habit of getting mad when he misses a free-throw, thereby reinforcing his error. Donny needed to change his Self-Image. His attitude needed to be, "I am the best free-throw shooter on the team."

You Must Be Willing To Change

One day Donny approached the coach. "OK, coach, I'm ready to do whatever it takes to make the starting squad. What do I have to do?"

"Are you ready to change your attitude about making free-throws?"

"Yes, coach, I'm ready!"

You Must Identify The Attitudes and Habits You Need To Change

How do you identify which habits and attitudes you need to change? It is easier than you think. Simply look at the problems you are having and start there. If you turn your weaknesses into strengths, your performance will surely benefit. In this regard, problems and frustrations are valuable keys to your success. For skilled athletes and business professionals, most of the time their problems are negative attitudes and poor reinforcement.

In our example, Donny needs to change one attitude and one habit. The attitude that needs changing is his opinion of himself, "I'm not a good free-throw shooter." Also, he must eliminate reinforcing his missed shots.

Set Up A New Self-Image That Is In Direct Conflict With Your Old Habits and Attitudes

Donny's new attitude is, "I am the best free-throw shooter on my team." His new habit is each time he makes a free-throw he must say, "That's like me!" Each time he misses he must forget his error. Olympic athletes call this technique Feast or Forget. He must run a mental program on each free-throw to maximize his chance of making every shot. He should reinforce his successes by recording in his Performance Analysis Journal.

Exchange Your Old Self-Image For The Desired New One

Replacing an old Self-Image with a new one is no simple matter. Our habits and attitudes were instilled over a long period of time and are not easily dislodged. The mental process that I endorse is both safe and extremely effective. It is called the Directive Affirmation.

Chapter 14
The Directive Affirmation

Shortly before the 1976 Olympics, I developed the Directive Affirmation that we teach today. I credit it with having the greatest single impact on building the Self-Image necessary for my success in athletics and business. Once you have mastered this Mental Management® tool, you can change any habit or attitude that you do not like about yourself normally within 21 days. You can use the Directive Affirmation to help you achieve anything you desire in your life. This concept is not magic but certainly seems to work like it. I used this tool to win the 1976 Olympics and the World Championships in 1978.

The Directive Affirmation is effective for increasing productivity, reducing the negative effects of stress and creating winning attitudes.

It is a paragraph written in the first person present tense that describes a person's goal, pay-value of the goal, plan to reach a goal and the habits and attitudes affecting the goal. It is rehearsed repetitively, causing the Self-Image to change.

To illustrate how the tool works, we will use the example of Donny, the basketball player.

Writing A Directive Affirmation

Step 1: Define the goal: In Donny's case, it was to become the best free-throw shooter on this team. He would write it as, "I am the best free-throw shooter on my team."

Step 2: Set a time limit: Donny would run the Directive Affirmation for 21 days from the start date.

Step 3: List the personal pay-value to reach the goal: Donny would write, "I am a starter on the basketball team. I help my team win because I score well at the free-throw line."

Step 4: Outline a plan to achieve the goal: run a mental program before each free-throw in practice and in games. Every time I score I say, "That's Like Me!" If I do not score, I immediately focus on the next shot or the next play. Record my Performance Analysis daily. Read and visualize my Directive Affirmations daily.

Step 5: Write a Directive Affirmation in the first person present tense, beginning with the word "I." State the goal as if you already are in possession of it. Next list the pay-value. List your plan to reach your goal. Restate the goal. Date the paragraph with your target date.

Donny's Directive Affirmation might be:

11/21/_____. I am the best free-throw shooter on my team. I start each game and enjoy the chance to help my team win by making free-throws. I always run a mental program before each shot and reinforce each successful basket by saying, "That's like me." Then I focus on the next shot or play. Also, I record my Performance Analysis and read and visualize my Directive Affirmation daily. I am the best free-throw shooter on my team.

Step 6: Make five copies of the Directive Affirmation in your own handwriting on five-by-seven file cards.

Step 7: Place the cards in five prominent places, such as your bathroom mirror, on the refrigerator door, on your desk, on your computer terminal, on the bedroom door, as a bookmark in the book you are reading. These places are called key points.

Step 8: Read and visualize your Directive Affirmation each time you come to a key point. A key point is a suitable location for a Directive Affirmation card. It should be a place that you visit often in your normal day. Each time Donny comes to a key point, he must read and visualize the Directive Affirmation, seeing himself as the person in the Directive Affirmation. Run the Directive Affirmation for twenty-one days, then remove it and rest for nine days. Then you may modify the previous Directive Affirmation; or, if totally satisfied with the results, replace it; or, if you need more time, repeat the same Directive Affirmation. Soon, as your Self-Image changes, you will become the person described in the Directive Affirmation. Your performance will automatically improve.

When Donny begins to read the Directive Affirmation, he sees himself as being the best free-throw shooter on his team. He pictures starting every game and making a contribution to his team. He sees himself running a mental program, sinking the basket, and saying, "That's like me!" Donny records his successes in his Performance Journal and reads and visualizes his Directive Affirmations daily. Each session should only take a few minutes.

This is not the way Donny has thought of himself in the past. This new Self-Image is in direct conflict with his old Self-Image. The Self-Image cannot stand conflict. Something has to go; it will be the new Self-Image or the old one. As Donny continues to imprint the "new Donny" in the Directive Affirmation, at some point the conflict is resolved by the exchange of the old attitudes and habits with the news ones. Wham. The Self-Image is changed, and Donny starts sinking free-throws.

Reshaping the mind is much like reshaping the physical body. If you are overweight, it is likely that the cause is repetitive overeating. Repetitive change of your eating habits is the best way to bring your weight down safely. If you have a poor attitude, it is likely that the cause is repetitive negative reinforcement. Repetitive change of your thinking habits is the best way to bring about an attitude change.

The real power in the Directive Affirmation is that it requires the user to set a goal, list a pay-value, set a time limit, identify a plan to get the goal by changing an attitude or habit (or both), and repeat over and over each day a new positive picture.

Does this sound familiar? You know that you should do these things, but unless there is a way to require yourself to do them, you won't! How many times have you read a self-improvement book or attended a seminar, then you came home all excited, but two weeks later you were the same old person? If any change occurred in you at all, it was temporary.

The Directive Affirmation is a tool to affect permanent change. If you follow the steps in the Directive Affirmation carefully, there are only two possible outcomes. Either you will become the person you want to be or you will stop reading the affirmation. It is that simple.

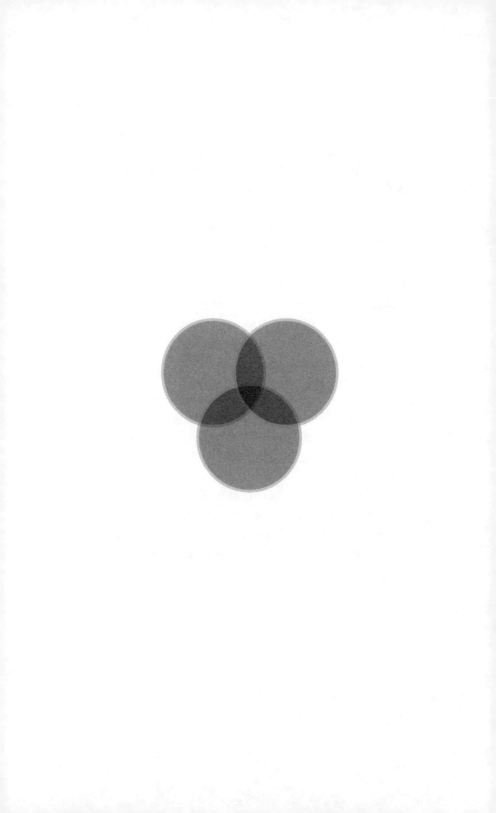

Chapter 15
Making the Directive Affirmation Work for You

In more than 35 years experience using and teaching the Directive Affirmation, I have seen phenomenal results in a broad range of applications. In this chapter, I will list several examples of the Directive Affirmation at work.

Directive Affirmation For Weight Control

People are not successful in dieting because they have their goal stated incorrectly. If you are ten pounds overweight, the goal should not be to lose ten pounds – it should be to lose the weight and keep it off. Instead, you go on your favorite diet. This normally means you alter your eating habits. This is not like you, and your old Self-Image begins to fight you from the very beginning. Still, you persist, and after some time you notice a drop of a few pounds. Since your goal is to lose ten pounds, you continue until you are ten pounds lighter. Then an amazing thing happens. For you to continue to reach your goal of losing weight, you must gain weight again. Soon you are ten pounds heavier again. The cycle then repeats.

You can lose a thousand pounds with this method, gain ten, then lose it to gain again.

A better way is to set the correct goal. If you weigh 170 and want to weigh 160, then set the goal to maintain a fit 160-pound weight.

Let's set up a Directive Affirmation to achieve the desired body weight. Using the Directive Affirmation, you will find that your diet is easier to follow, and you will experience a change in Self-Image.

You should not have to lose weight again.

Step 1: Define the goal: To weigh 160 pounds.

Step 2: Set a time limit: Two months from now.

Step 3: List the personal pay-value to reach the goal. "I feel better and look better at 160. I can wear my best suit comfortably."

Step 4: Outline a plan to achieve the goal:

Eat a high-protein, low-fat diet. Drink a food supplement shake or eat a food bar for lunch. Program and prepare nutritious meals in advance. Exercise daily for at least 45 minutes. Read and rehearse my Directive Affirmations daily for 21 days.

Step 5: Write a Directive Affirmation.

11/1/12. I weigh 160 pounds. I feel and look great at 160. I enjoy wearing my best suit in comfort. I eat a high-protein, low-fat diet. I drink a food supplement shake instead of lunch three times a week. I program and prepare nutritious meals in advance. I exercise daily for at least 45 minutes. I read and rehearse my Directive Affirmations daily. I weigh 160 pounds.

Directive Affirmation To Become A Non-Smoker

Many smokers find it difficult to stop smoking and not return to their old Self-Image of being a smoker. Again, the difficulty is due to setting the wrong goal. The goal should not be to stop smoking, the goal should be to become a non-smoker. If your goal is to stop smoking, to attain your goal, it is necessary to begin smoking again. You stop, then start, then stop, then start again. There is a better way. With the Directive Affirmation, change is permanent.

Step 1: Define the goal: To become a non-smoker.

Step 2: Set a time limit: Twenty-one days from now.

Step 3: List the personal pay-value to reach the goal. "I have prolonged endurance, more energy, and longer life expectancy."

Step 4: Outline a plan to achieve the goal:

I allow no cigarettes in my home. I chew gum when I feel like smoking. I say continually, "I control my life, not a chemical." Read and visualize my Directive Affirmations daily for twenty-one days.

Step 5: Write a Directive Affirmation.

11/1/11. I enjoy being a non-smoker. I feel strong and healthy, with more energy. I know I will live longer. I permit no cigarettes in my home. I chew gum when needed, and continually say, "I control my life, not a chemical." I read and rehearse my Directive Affirmations daily. I enjoy being a non-smoker.

Directive Affirmation For Making Olympic Shooting Team

I thought you might like to see the Directive Affirmation I utilized to make the Olympic team in 1976. The same format can be used for any high-level goal for competition.

Step 1: Define the goal: To become a member of the 1976 U.S. Olympic Shooting Team.

Step 2: Set a time limit: By 1 July 1976.

Step 3: List the personal pay-value to reach the

goal. "I have taken the next step toward winning the Olympic Games. I enjoy the recognition of being one of the best shooters in my country. I have qualified for an all-expense paid trip to Montreal, Canada, to compete for the Olympic gold medal."

Step 4: Outline a plan to achieve the goal:

Preload before each stage, run a mental program on each shot, reload each shot (Editor's Note: advanced mental techniques developed by Lanny outside the scope of this text), record my Performance Analysis daily, and rehearse the appropriate mental and technical process several times each day. Train five days a week, five hours a day, using progressive training of dry firing, group shooting, and match simulation. Jog three miles four times a week. Supplement my diet with Nutrilite XX daily. Read and rehearse my Directive Affirmations daily.

Step 5: Write a Directive Affirmation.

1/1/76. I am a member of the 1976 U.S. Olympic Shooting Team. I have taken my next step toward the accomplishment of my lifelong goal, an Olympic Gold Medal.

I enjoy the recognition as one of the best shooters in my country. I look forward to the all-expense-paid trip to Montreal to compete at the Games.

I always preload before each stage, run a mental program on each shot, reload each shot, record my Performance Analysis daily, and rehearse experiencing being in the Olympics and running the appropriate mental and technical process several times each day. Train five days a week, five hours a day, using progressive training of dry firing, group shooting, and match simulation. I jog three miles, four times a week, and eat my Nutrilite XX food supplement daily. I read and rehearse my Directive Affirmations daily. I am member of the 1976 U.S. Olympic Shooting Team.

Directive Affirmation For Remembering Names

Occasionally, we need an affirmation to change something about ourselves that we do not like. Some of us are poor at remembering names. The major reason why people cannot remember the names of others is that they have poor name-remembering habits. When most of us meet a new person, we do not even hear their name. We are too busy saying our own name. If you will implement the following habits, you will become skilled at recalling names. This Directive Affirmation should make you good at remembering names for the rest of your life.

Step 1: Define the goal: To become good at remembering names.

Step 2: Set a time limit: One month from today.

Step 3: List the personal pay-value to reach the goal. I feel good when I can remember a person's name. They feel good as well. Remembering names is good for business.

Step 4: Outline a plan to achieve the goal:

When I meet a new person I repeat their name, spell it, form an association with their name and later write it down.

Step 5: Write a Directive Affirmation.

6/1/11. I am good at remembering names. When I recall a new person's name, it makes me feel good. It also makes them feel good, and it is good for business. When I meet a new person, I always repeat their name, spell it, form an association, and later write it down. I am good at remembering names.

Directive Affirmation For Becoming A Better Time Manager

Time may be the only asset you cannot recover once it is lost. Becoming a good time manager should be high on any successful person's list of skills. There are many useful books available on time management. Many people find implementing the suggestions in these books difficult. The Directive Affirmation is just the tool to solve this difficulty.

Step 1: Define the goal: To become a good time manger.

Step 2: Set a time limit: Twenty-one days out.

Step 3: List the personal pay-value to reach the goal. "I feel organized. I get many things done in a short time. I can find the information I am looking for easily."

Step 4: Outline a plan to achieve the goal:

I keep all my notes, calendars, addresses, and schedules in a journal that I always keep with me. I write out a things-to-do list before the beginning of each day, ranking each item and scheduling the most important first. I keep a clear desk and work on only one item at a time.

Step 5: Write a Directive Affirmation.

8/1/11. I am a good manager of my time. I am well organized, getting things done in an efficient, timely manner. I can find information that I am looking for easily. I keep all my notes, calendar, addresses, and schedules in a journal that I always keep with me.

I write out a things-to-do list before the beginning of each day, ranking each item, and scheduling the most important first. I keep a clear desk and work on only one item at a time. I am a good manager of my time.

Directive Affirmation To Become Debt Free

You can even use the Directive Affirmation to help with the bills. We live in a day of credit cards and easy credit. With the inflating costs of homes and autos, it is no wonder that most people must deal with more and more debt. The major reason more people are not debt-free is that they never goal-set to become debt-free. We often goal-set to increase our income, but when the income increases, we simply increase our "wants". The Directive Affirmation can help. You should only set a goal that you can accomplish in 21 days. Becoming debt-free might take much longer than this time period. Here is the answer; begin the goal with the words "I am on my way." You can be "on your way" to accomplishing your goals within the 21 day time period. Use this technique for any goal that takes longer than 21 days to reach.

Step 1: Define the goal: To become debt-free. To owe no one.

Step 2: Set a time limit: Within two to five years

of today's date. Run for the twenty-one days, rest nine, repeat if necessary. (Remember, you only have to use the Directive Affirmation until your Self-Image changes. Then, if you continue focusing on the goal, your Subconscious will provide the power to achieve it).

Step 3: List the personal pay-value to reach the goal. "Debt equals stress. Imagine a life with no mortgage, no credit card balances, no loans outstanding, and no fear of bankruptcy."

Step 4: Outline a plan to achieve the goal:

If the goal is more than one year away, as in this case, focus on a key objective that is along the goal's path. You may have to move through three or four objectives to achieve your long-term goal.

Invest ten percent of all you earn in an interest-bearing program. Stop all charge card and credit purchases, paying with cash or check. Set up a budget to live on less than you earn, apply the balance to reducing debt. Aggressively seek out opportunity to increase your income, applying the increase toward the debt.

Step 5: Write a Directive Affirmation.

12/1/11. I am on my way to becoming debt-free.

I pay no interest. I have no mortgage, no credit card balances, and no loans due. I am financially free. I invest ten percent of everything I earn in an interest-bearing program. I pay cash for what I purchase. I set up a budget to live on less than I earn, applying the difference towards reducing debt. I aggressively seek out opportunities to increase my income, applying a portion of the increase toward the debt. I am debt free.

Directive Affirmation For Passing Exams

For students who are concerned about finals, or professionals who are concerned about state boards, this Directive Affirmation will make you a better test-taker.

Step 1: Define the goal: To make an A on the final exam in Mental Management® 101.

Step 2: Set a time limit: The exam date.

Step 3: List the personal pay-value to reach the goal: "Passing the exam is necessary for passing the course. I will have taken a vital step toward graduation. I will enjoy the feeling of scoring high on the exam."

Step 4: Outline a plan to achieve the goal:

I prepare for classes by reading the assigned text before class and finishing the homework. I take good notes in class. I study adequately for the final. I rehearse taking the final, knowing the answers, and scoring well. I read and visualize my Directive Affirmation daily.

Step 5: Write a Directive Affirmation.

12/1/11. I made an A on my final exam in Mental Management® 101. I enjoy the feeling of making a top grade on this final. I have passed the course and taken a vital step towards graduation from the Thrill of Victory University. I prepared for the final by reading the assigned text, turning in my homework in a timely manner, taking good notes, and studying for the exams. I rehearsed taking the final, knowing the answers, and scoring well. I read and rehearse my Directive Affirmation daily. I made an A on my final exam in Mental Management® 101.

Directive Affirmation For Starting Your Own Business

A Directive Affirmation can be written for any goal, even if you are unsure of a plan to acquire the goal. Here is an example a student of mine used to start his own business.

Step 1: Define the goal: To start my own business with a higher salary than I presently earn, without having to move from the city.

Step 2: Set a time limit: Six months from now.

Step 3: List the personal pay-value to reach the goal: "More money to enhance my lifestyle. Change in job eliminates burn-out. I enjoy the feeling of moving upward in my community. I control my finances."

Step 4: Outline a plan to achieve the goal:

Look for a way to start a better paying business. Rehearse beginning a new business with higher pay. Read and visualize my Directive Affirmation daily.

Step 5: Write a Directive Affirmation.

12/1/11. I enjoy running my new business here in my community. I enjoy the feeling of moving up in my financial position. I am excited about the increased income I am receiving. I created this new business by staying open to any new idea that would increase my income, rehearsing that I created a higher-paying business in the city, and reading and rehearsing my Directive Affirmations daily. I enjoy running my new business here in my community.

Now write a Directive Affirmation for your goal, using the examples in this chapter. Follow the checks below to ensure you have written the affirmation correctly.

Is the goal one you want personally? Is it exciting to you? Did you place the time limit at least twenty-one days and no more than four years from today's date? Goals that are more than four years in the future must be fragmented into objectives that you can work on within the near future.

Do your goals create a conflict between your current Self-Image and the Self-Image you wish to acquire?

Did you begin with the word I?

Did you write the statements in the first person present or past tense? Be careful not to use future tense such as "I want to win the national championships," or "I plan to win the national champions." Instead write, "I am the national champion."

Did you write a statement describing the pay-value to you for achieving the goal?

Did you write a statement detailing how you plan to achieve the goal?

Did you repeat the goal statement?

Follow these guidelines, and you will be able to write an effective Directive Affirmation for your goals.

Chapter 16
Decisiveness

Decisiveness is the noun form of the adjective decisive and it is a powerful quality to have on your side when competing. One definition of the word is 'having the power to determine an outcome beyond doubt.' Wow. Decisiveness is power. How does that sound? Decisiveness is also a decision that once made alters the very fabric of the performer's Self-Image in the contest. It empowers the person to perform at the very top of their technical skill. You can see the dramatic effect of this decision in the best performers when they enter the arena. Without conscious effort their posture seems to change. Their shoulders seem to set a little straighter and the chin lifts just a bit. The eyes seem to have a quiet focus on the task and you can almost hear them thinking "This is going to be a great day!" They can feel the energy begin to radiate through their movements. There is a feeling that they have been here before and all will go well. There is trust in both their skill and in their ability to reproduce great performances. This confidence is beyond conscious thought and cannot be faked. It is available only to the prepared performer. It is a weapon against failure that knows few equals. It is the advantage of the resolved and the edge of the determined. Yet, you are not born with it. No one can give it to you. No one can do it for you. It is priceless but you cannot buy it. No matter how hard you work you cannot earn it. It is invisible yet everyone can see it in those who have it. It comes easiest to the skilled and evades those that seek the easy path to success. It is available to everyone yet few have it and it is one characteristic that you cannot afford to do without. If you want it there is only one way to get it. You make a decision and it is there.

So, would you ever wish to be indecisive, to give up this huge advantage and risk failure? You would think not, but it happens way too often in competitions. Although there may be dozens of reasons that this can occur, I believe that there are three primary reasons for lack of decisiveness. We might become indecisive because we are new to the sport, ill-prepared for the event or overly-cautious in our planning. Let's take a look at these one at a time.

Are you new to the sport? Everyone is a novice in the beginning, and it is perhaps impossible for us to be very decisive when we start anything new. I have a few suggestions though. View your first few competitions ONLY as learning experiences. Evaluate what you are doing well and in the next event be decisive about what you know you can do correctly. As your skill and execution improves you will have more to become decisive about and you may find that you will gain confidence in all areas of your performance. We find that new performers often focus too much on what they are doing wrong and do not give themselves enough credit in the areas that they are doing well. Trying not to make a mistake is a sure way of making one. All attempts are teaching platforms. Remember to reinforce what you are doing well after each attempt as you are learning to correct error.

Next, and this is applicable to veterans as well as newcomers, discipline yourself to only think and talk about what you need to do – not about what you did when referring to your performance. Talking about what you need to do builds Self-Image but talking about error tends to tear it down. A statement like "I need to be more decisive," is an aid to your Self-Image growth but "I'm just not decisive," reinforces error.

Also, remember the best time to ask for help is in the beginning. Most of the more experienced competitors are quick to help you but you need to let them know that you need their help most of the time. Remember, we are happy you are here and we want to encourage you.

Now, do not wait until you feel you are totally prepared to begin competing. Perfection is the purest form of procrastination. There are some things you can only learn by competing. Sooner or later you will get to a position that is beyond your current skill level. It is really difficult to be decisive here. Human nature is telling you to worry about this upcoming challenge and a bit of trepidation sets in. My suggestion is to work the problem. All you can do is perform with what you have brought with you. You are not going to manufacture anything new at this point but you must be careful not to let the concern over this issue cause your performance to deteriorate. Stay strong in your attitude about what you can do.

When driving in bad weather we exercise caution. When we have to move around in the dark we are cautious. If we have to make a big decision we are taught by our mentors to use caution. Normally caution is a good thing but too much of it can paralyze a performer. There is a fine line between indecision and caution. A cautious person carefully weighs options but the focus is on how best to accomplish the task. An indecisive person is worried about making the wrong decision.

Remember "having the power to determine an outcome beyond doubt" is like you. Work the problem, decisively execute your technical and mental systems and your performance will tend to meet your expectation.

Chapter 17
Become a Promoter

My father often told a story about a cowboy in a bar who was continually bragging to the bartender about the quality of his horse.

"My horse is the best-looking, best-trained, smartest animal in the state!"

"I'd like to buy a horse like that. How much is he?" asked the bartender.

"Not for sale at any price. Everyone says he's the finest horse they have ever seen. I'm just proud to own him."

Finally, the bartender could not stand it any more and offered the cowboy such a high price that a sale was made. The next day the bartender was furious when he came to the bar.

"Where is that cheat who sold me the horse!" the bartender raved. Then he spotted the cowboy and remarked.

"The animal you sold me is lame, ugly, untrained, and worthless. You can't ride him. He's cross-eyed and sway-backed. What do you have to say for yourself, cowboy?"

"I've just one thing to say," the cowboy drawled,

"If you don't quit cutting down that horse, you ain't never going to sell him."

A great word in the English language is "promotion." The cowboy was successful because he was a good promoter. Webster defines promote as "to raise or move forward to a higher or better position, to further the growth of something, or to work actively, stirring up interest in an idea or concept." This is a powerful word. A good mental manager is a promoter. I suggest three areas we should promote: our systems, ourselves and the Self-Image growth of others.

Promoting Systems

I am not an expert in politics, but I suggest that if we had a society filled with people promoting the country, instead of verbally tearing it down, we could achieve greater things as a nation. We must loudly champion the things that are right about our system, while silently going about changing the things that are wrong. Too many times, it is the other way around.

Athletes should promote their national associations and national governing bodies. We must promote our coaches, team administrators, and managers. I spent twenty years as an athlete, ten of those years on the U.S. national team. Most of my life I have been a coach, teacher, administrator, and a parent of athletes. I have gained a tremendous respect

166

for those supporting sports activities. When I competed, I am certain that I was not always supportive of the people who ran the matches, the organizers, or the administrators. I could not fully appreciate the difficulty of their tasks until I had walked in their shoes.

If you are in business, you must praise your profession, your industry, your company, your product as well as those you work for and with. Gold medals are never won alone.

If you are a parent of an athlete, I respect you for sacrificing for your children. I am the father of three. My boys are twins and both have been involved in shooting. My daughter competed in pageants. I remember buying things, carrying things and driving them to competitions.

If you are a coach, I respect you for your diligence. When the team wins, everyone says, "The athletes did it." When it loses, they say, "It's the fault of the coach." Most of the coaches I know are volunteers. Their only reward is the occasional praise they receive. They are never paid enough.

Finally, and most important, we must not forget the role played by the wives and husbands of the champions. The cost for an Olympic gold medal is great, especially for the spouse. After winning my gold medal, many people surrounded me at the functions my wife and I attended. One day, I noticed that they had pushed Helen away from me. She was not seen as an important factor in the win. All they wanted was the medalist. I stopped the interview, joined my wife, and held her close.

For three years prior to my first Olympics, I spent more nights away from my family than I did at home. Helen squeezed every penny out of our budget for extra ammunition. We never went on a vacation, we always took my vacation time at another rifle match. She did not complain. The gold medal is ours, together. By the way, at sometime you will have to pay them back. I am in the payback period now but happy to do it.

Promoting Ourselves

It has become socially acceptable in our society to present ourselves as being less than acceptable when we speak to others. Recently, I heard a lady compliment another woman, saying, "What a nice dress!" Her friend answered, "What, this old thing?"

You cannot expect people to think well of you if you are not willing to think well of yourself. I am not saying that we should boast. But I have had just about enough of people apologizing for being competent. I can assure you the Olympic champions I know do not hold their heads down when a compliment is offered. Do not be afraid of accepting the sincere praise offered by others. Say "Thank You." out loud, and say silently to yourself, "That's like me." The best way to promote yourself is to control your self-talk. Say, "I am getting better at that." rather than "I always do poorly."

You can promote inner growth by feeding your mind positive information through reading and listening. I encourage you to listen to recordings of motivational speakers while you drive your car. Your library is full of books on the subjects of being positive, self-improvement, and personal growth. Reading is a wonderful way to inherit the success of the writers. Make your mind a depository of positive information. Email me for a list of my recommended books at info@mentalmanagement.com.

Promoting Others

Building Self-Image in others is a primary task of parents, teachers, and coaches. I offer six simple suggestions to promote the growth of your students and children.

Look them in the eye. When you are speaking or listening to someone, you are building them up when you look right at them. Conversely, you tear them down by looking away. Eye contact shows you are concerned about the other person and that you place a high value on the person you are speaking with.

A name is everything. Nicknames can build up or tear down. Ask yourself, is a name aiding or hindering a student? How does the student feel about the name? If they do not value the name, do not use it.

Many years ago, Helen and I selected what we thought was the most beautiful name we had ever heard for a little girl. That is how our daughter Heather Dawn got her name. When she was little, I called her "Heather-Belle" and Helen called her "Doodle." Now that she is an adult, "Doodle" just doesn't fit anymore. She will always be my Heather-Belle, I just won't call her that in front of anyone.

Praise in public, correct in private. No one is motivated by being chewed-out in front of peers. I see far too many coaches who break this rule. This practice tears down Self-Image. Public praise builds Self-Image.

Praise twice as much as you correct. Remember, you are building by praising. There is no question that corrections must be made in a tactful, timely manner. But you build Self-Image by promoting more often than you criticize.

Never steal a dream or limit a goal. My twin sons Brian and Troy were excellent soccer players when they were young. One summer, we saw an advertisement in the newspaper about a five-week, European/ Soviet soccer tour. The team would play in seven countries, including the Soviet Union. Tryouts were to be held in San Antonio, Houston, and Austin to select only 16 boys from the state of Texas. When Brian, Troy, and I arrived at the tryout, we discovered that the participants, once selected, would have to raise over $2,500 each to offset costs. When these facts were announced, over 75 percent of the boys walked off the field before try-outs began.

My sons came to me and said, "Dad, do you think

we have a chance to make this team? Should we try out?" I replied, "You can't win if you don't enter." They both made the team. It was a tremendous effort, but both boys raised $2,500 each from contributions made by local merchants and businesses in our little town of Seguin. Their dream was realized.

Never give up on anyone. In the 1950s and early 1960s, the U.S. Army Marksmanship Unit shooters began to dominate international shooting. During this period, one of the shooters stayed on the bench his first three years on the army team. He was unable to make the U.S. national team. The army questioned his ability; it seemed he just did not have what it took to become a champion.

The shooter resigned from the army, but he returned to active duty within a year of making the 1964 U.S. Olympic team. That year Lones Wigger Jr. won an Olympic gold medal, setting a new world record. Wigger is the most successful athlete in international competition in the history of this country. He has won more medals, made more U.S. teams, and set more world records than any other American in any sport.

The point: some people choose their own time to become a champion. Do not give the appearance that you have given up on your students or children. Also, giving up on yourself brings down your Self-Image faster than any other factor I know. Become a promoter of your organization, of yourself, and of others.

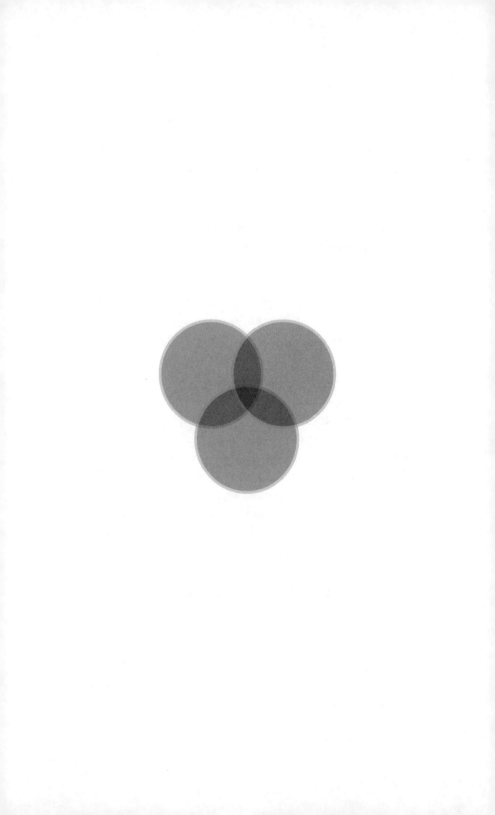

Chapter 18
The Challenge

D o you want to win? Do you want to win all of the time? Really? What if you did? What if every attempt was successful and nothing ever went wrong? What if it became way too easy to do? How long would it take for you to tire of it? Winning is special because it is so difficult to do. We tend to value things in direct proportion to the price we pay for them. We do not learn very much standing on the summit. All of the becoming happens on the way up the mountain. I hope you are having a lot of challenges along your journey of a dream. Resistance makes you stronger. If you are not having problems your goals are too low.

Principle of Mental Management® Number 9

The Principal Of Value: We appreciate things in direct proportion to the price we pay for them.

We learn more from the shots we miss than the ones we make. We are taught when we are growing up that making mistakes is costly and should be avoided. When papers are returned from our teachers in school with red marks around our mistakes we are reminded of these costs. But I submit to you that making the first mistake is rarely unavoidable. All elite performers have made countless mistakes when competing. The key is to discern what lessons these experiences are trying to teach us. The focus must be on learning from failure not thinking that you are a failure.

"Success does not consist in never making mistakes but in never making the same one a second time." - George Bernard Shaw

Performers struggle with this one every time they fail to win. In the reinforcement phase of an action the performer must determine the best course of action for the next attempt. Do not be afraid of making mistakes. John Maxwell once wrote, "The greatest mistake we make is living in constant fear that we will make one." If you are fearful of making a mistake your focus in a competition is on outcome not on process and your mental game will always be a variable. When your focus is on avoiding error the picture you are imprinting on your Self-Image is the error itself. Ninety percent of everything we worry about never happens and even when it does many times it is for our benefit.

The Challenge

I challenge you to take action. You live at a unique time in history. If you are a competitor I would bet that your competition while thinking that the mental game is critical to success is doing little to advance their mental game. What if you did? The fact that you are reading this book puts you ahead of the competition. How much ahead depends on the effort you put forth in applying it.

I challenge you to take action. Your competition is thinking the thoughts their environment gives them. This is typical. What if you were not typical? You have a choice to continue to allow your thoughts to be controlled by your environment or to control them yourself. Running a mental system means that you define the best things to think about before, during and after your stage of competition. What if you trained your Subconscious to respond consistently to these thoughts so that they were embedded? What if you trusted yourself to only think this way in competitions?

I challenge you to take action. Your competition, your friends, your parents, your bosses, your teachers do not understand that when they talk to you in a way that causes you to picture what you did wrong it becomes like you to repeat it. They do not understand that talking about what you did instead of what you should have done shatters your Self-Image. But, you do understand this now. What if your self-talk centered on what you need to do and not what you did? What if while others choose to beat themselves up you choose to build yourself up?

I challenge you to take action. Not everything is as it seems. There are times in our lives when our circumstances appear to us to be heading toward doom when in reality we are on the road to our dreams. We just don't realize it. I challenge you to look at problems and adversity as learning experiences, to see the potential lesson in every failure and to appreciate just how fortunate you are when you finish well. I challenge you to take successful outcomes as confirmation that you are on the right track and unsuccessful ones as opportunities to learn.

A friend of mine is a firefighter. He tells a story about a great apartment fire in the city. The fire spread so fast that the only way the people in the top floor could be saved was to place a ladder from the roof to the window of an adjacent building. The people were forced to crawl across the ladder to safety. The ladder was ten stories above the ground.

Everyone was saved except a woman and her six-year-old son. The woman was afraid of heights, so the fireman, at the risk of his life, crawled across the ladder, rescuing her son. From the window, the fireman called to the woman, "Come across now, the fire is close." She would not move. She kept looking down at the street below. He heard her say, "I would rather burn than fall!"

The fireman did the only thing he could have

done to save the woman. He took her son back across the ladder. He said, "If your son is to live, you are going to have to save him."

She did.

It was not like the woman to cross the ladder, but it was like her to save her son. You are in control of what you consciously think about, your subconscious skills, and your Self-Image growth. You have a ladder to cross. It is the ladder of mental control and it leads to your dreams.

Lanny Bassham, founder of Mental Management® Systems, is the driving force behind the creation of the mental strategies presented in the seminars and products offered by the company.

Lanny not only developed the Mental Management® System but also used it personally to win 35 medals in international rifle competition for the USA including 22 world individual and team titles, setting 4 world records, and winning the coveted Olympic Gold Medal in Montreal in 1976. This ranks him third in medal count for the USA among all shooters. Lanny is a member of the USA Shooting Hall of Fame. He lives in Flower Mound, Texas.

Contact him at 972-899-9640

Hear Lanny Bassham at your event.

Keynote Speeches include:

Freedom Flight - The Origins of Mental Power - a powerful 45 min. to 1 hour message on controlling your mind in spite of your environment. How to keep your mind focused on what is important and letting the unimportant go. This story is based on a true event where Lanny met someone who changed his life and direction forever. This story is also available in book or audio CD. We offer bulk discounts to companies who hire Lanny to speak.

When Silver is Not Enough - a 20 minute to 1 hour talk based on Lanny's personal story of the boy who couldn't make the team and was picked last in every sport to Olympic Champion. Throughout the story of his life Lanny tells several principles of success that can be applied to any business situation.

To learn more about how Mental Management® can help you in your sport or business please call 972-899-9640 or you may also send an email to info@mentalmanagement. com and we will be happy to assist you.

WITH WINNING IN MIND
(200 page BOOK 3rd edition)
The book that started it all, great for anyone interested in having a consistent mental performance under pressure. The book introduces Mental Management® and is packed with techniques for competitors. Learn how performance is a function of three mental processes, how to control the mind under pressure and how to train for competition. Unlock the secrets of Olympic Champions.

WITH WINNING IN MIND
(AUDIO CD - includes 4 audio CDs)
With Winning In Mind is great for anyone interested in having a consistent mental performance under pressure. The book introduces Mental Management® and is packed with techniques for competitors. Learn how performance is a function of three mental processes, how to control the mind under pressure and how to train for competition. Unlock the secrets of Olympic Champions.

LANNY BASSHAM

FREEDOM FLIGHT
The Origins of Mental Power

An Olympic Medalist has a life-changing conversation
with a man on a plane ride to Cairo that will forever
change his chances of success
in sport and in life

Olympic Silver Medalist, Lanny Bassham, was feeling truly defeated and sorry for himself due to his failure to reach his ultimate goal. He meets a man who changes his perspective, his attitude and most importantly his future. An unlikely mentor named Jack explains to Lanny that he is has lost his freedom and is living in a self-imposed prison. During their plane flight to Cairo, these two strangers embark on a truly inspirational discovery. Inspired by true events this 96 page book includes 14 success principles and packs a powerful punch to those who choose to experience the flight of their life – their Freedom Flight. Take back your freedom, break down the walls to your self-imposed prison and reach for your dreams.

Order at 972-899-9640

www.mentalmanagement.com